S0-EFM-123

The Tragedy of

ROMEO AND JULIET

with Related Readings

SERIES EDITORS

Dom Saliani   Chris Ferguson   Dr. Tim Scott

I(T)P *International Thomson Publishing*

Albany • Bonn • Boston • Cincinnati • Detroit • London • Madrid • Melbourne • Mexico City
New York • Pacific Grove • Paris • San Francisco • Singapore • Tokyo • Toronto • Washington

International Thomson Publishing, 1997

All rights in this book are reserved.
The text of this publication, or any part thereof, may not be reproduced or transmitted in any form or by any means, electronic or mechanical, including photocopying, storage in an information retrieval system, or otherwise, without the prior written permission of the publisher.

The trademark ITP is used under licence.

Published simultaneously in 1997 by International Thomson Limited:

ITP Nelson (Canada)   **South-Western Educational Publishing (U.S.A.)**
Nelson ITP (Australia)   **Thomas Nelson United Kingdom**

http://www.thomson.com

ISBN-13: 978-0-17-606613-0
ISBN-10: 0-17-606613-6

Cataloguing in Publication Data

Shakespeare, William, 1564-1616
      [Romeo and Juliet]
    The tragedy of Romeo and Juliet with related readings

(The global Shakespeare series)
ISBN 0-17-606613-6

1. Shakespeare, William, 1564-1616.   Romeo
and Juliet.   I. Title.   II. Series.

PR2831.A1   1997   822.3'3   C97-930213-7

Acquisition Editor:	TARA STEELE
Project Managers:	JAN HARKNESS (CANADA)
	JACKIE TIDEY (AUSTRALIA)
	LAURIE WENDELL (U.S.A.)
Series Designer:	LIZ HARASYMCZUK
Cover Illustrator:	YUAN LEE
Production Editors:	KAREN ALLISTON, KATHLEEN FFOLLIOTT,
	SANDRA MANLEY
Composition Analyst:	DARYN DEWALT
Production Coordinator:	DONNA BROWN
Permissions Editor:	VICKI GOULD
Research:	LISA BRANT
Film:	IMAGING EXCELLENCE

Printed and bound in Canada
14 15 16 ITI 11 10 09

Contents

Features of the *Global Shakespeare Series*

Introduction to the Play: Information on the date, sources, themes, and appeal of the play, notes on Shakespeare's use of verse and prose, and common stage directions set a context for the play.

The Text: The *Global Shakespeare Series* is faithful to Shakespeare's full original texts. Spelling and punctuation have been modernized to make the plays more accessible to today's readers. For the last 200 years, many editors have chosen to arrange and rearrange Shakespeare's words to create a consistent iambic pentameter in the text. For example, a dialogue involving short speeches would look like this:

BENVOLIO: Good morrow, cousin.
ROMEO: Is the day so young?

Together the two lines make up 10 syllables. In some cases, editors have even taken words from one line and combined them with words from another line to create the iambic pentameter pattern. Shakespeare did not do this in his original text. The *Global Shakespeare Series* has not adopted this convention. What you see is what Shakespeare wrote.

Dramatis Personae: The list of characters is organized by families or by loyalty affiliations.

Scene Summaries: Brief synopses help you to follow and anticipate developments in the plot.

Artwork and Graphics: Original artwork has been created and designed for this series by internationally acclaimed artists.

Marginal Notes: Generous notes define difficult or archaic vocabulary. In some cases, entire sentences of Shakespeare are paraphrased into modern idiom — these are identified with quotation marks.

Notes of Interest: Longer notes provide background information on Shakespeare's times or interesting interpretations of various speeches or characters.

Quotable Notables: Brief comments on various aspects of the play by authors, celebrities, and highly regarded literary critics and professors are included. The views do not necessarily reflect the views of the editors; they are merely springboards for discussion, debate, and reflection.

Related Reading References: These references indicate that there is a piece of literature in the latter part of the book that relates well to a specific scene or speech.

Considerations: Each Act is followed by a series of scene-specific "considerations." Some involve analysis and interpretation; others offer opportunities to be creative and imaginative.

Related Readings: The second half of the text contains poems, short stories, short drama, and nonfiction pieces that are directly related to the play. These can be read for enjoyment and enrichment. They emphasize the continuing relevance of Shakespeare in today's society.

The 10 Most Challenging Questions: These questions are ideal for developing into research or independent study projects.

Introduction to
Romeo and Juliet

Appeal of *Romeo and Juliet*

Romeo and Juliet is one of the world's best-known love stories. For over four hundred years, readers and theatre audiences all over the world have been moved by this tragic story of young love. One of Shakespeare's most often performed plays, its continuing appeal is evident in the number of feature film versions and stage adaptations that continue to be produced and enjoyed by international audiences.

Romeo and Juliet appeals to us because it speaks of boundless passion and true love — a love that triumphs even over death. Juliet's words eloquently capture the essence of what it means to be in love:

> *My bounty is as boundless as the sea,*
> *My love as deep. The more I give to thee,*
> *The more I have, for both are infinite.*
> (2.2.139–141)

Romeo and Juliet is much more than a story about love. It is a play of contrasts: love and hate, joy and sorrow, light and dark, youth and age, life and death.

Why do people never tire of *Romeo and Juliet*? Perhaps its lasting appeal can be attributed to the play's unforgettable characters, its gripping plot, its universal themes, and its lyrical poetry.

Romeo and Juliet as Tragedy

Some critics argue that *Romeo and Juliet* is not a true tragedy. They suggest that the play is a variation of a form of drama called Tragedy of Fate that was popular during the early Elizabethan period. In such works, heroes are given great happiness in the beginning of the story and then are reduced to sorrow and ruin. Their fall is not their own fault. Rather, they are innocent victims of a seemingly malicious and unrelenting fate. The opening lines of *Romeo and Juliet* speak of an "ancient grudge" into which the "star-crossed" or ill-fated lovers are born. Furthermore, all through the story, there is evidence that the lovers' tragic demise occurs because of coincidence and misunderstanding — fate. This, critics suggest, disqualifies the play from being considered a true tragedy.

Proponents of this view will admit that the play contains tragic figures. For it to be considered a tragedy, however, it is argued that there needs to be evidence that the story contains heroes who come to a tragic end because of some fault in character and as the result of deliberate choice — not as a result of fate or coincidence.

Other critics, adhering to an opposite point of view, argue that the play is a true tragedy and that Romeo and Juliet hasten to their deaths specifically because of personality flaws. It is character and not fate that propels them toward their doom.

Are Romeo and Juliet innocent victims of fate and a fatal feud, or are they tragic heroes who succumb because of their excessive infatuatio and reckless rashness?

Sources of the Play

The earliest version of the story of Romeo and Juliet, which first appeared in 1476, claims that the story is true. Variations on the story, however, occur as far back as the fifth century B.C.E. In 1530 Luigi da Porto set the tragedy in Verona during the time of Bartolommeo della Scala (Escalus) and established the basic characters and storyline. In 1554 Matteo Bandello added a few characters and filled out the plot. In 1562 Arthur Brooke translated Bandello's story into English. Brooke's translation, a long, narrative poem titled *Romeus and Juliet* (3020 lines), is recognized as being Shakespeare's primary source for his play.

Shakespeare was quite faithful to the basic plot and characters as established by Brooke. He made some significant changes, however. For example, in Brooke's poem, Juliet is 16, she falls in love with Romeo at Christmas, and they die three months later at Easter. In Shakespeare's play, Juliet is not yet 14, and the time is compressed to span a mere five days. Shakespeare's characterization of Mercutio is also original, and the Paris subplot is almost all Shakespeare.

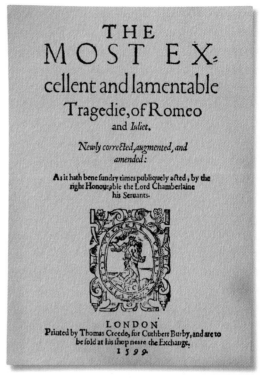

Title page of *Romeo and Juliet* from the Second Quarto, 1599

Date and Publications of the Play

Shakespeare wrote at least 37 plays. Of these, 18 appeared in *quarto* form. A quarto is a book produced by folding large sheets into four before binding the sheets together.

Romeo and Juliet first appeared in print in 1597 in a "bad" Quarto. That is, an actor put together a version of the play based on the actor's memory of it and sold this unauthorized version to an unscrupulous printer. This inferior First Quarto was displaced two years later with the publication of the "good" Second Quarto. Editors usually base their texts on the Second Quarto. The First Quarto, however, is often consulted for its more detailed stage directions.

THE TRAGEDIE OF
ROMEO and IVLIET.

Actus Primus. Scœna Prima.

Enter Sampson and Gregory, with Swords and Bucklers, of the House of Capulet.

Sampson.

Gregory: A my word wee'l not carry coales.
Greg. No, for then we should be Colliars.
Samp. I mean, if we be in choller, wee'l draw.
Greg. I, While you liue, draw your necke out o'th Collar.
Samp. I strike quickly, being mou'd.
Greg. But thou art not quickly mou'd to strike.
Samp. A dog of the house of *Mountague*, moues me.
Greg. To moue, is to stir: and to be valiant, is to stand: Therefore, if thou art mou'd, thou runst away.
Samp. A dogge of that house shall moue me to stand. I will take the wall of any Man or Maid of *Mountagues*.
Greg. That shewes thee a weake slaue, for the weakest goes to the wall.
Samp. True, and therefore women being the weaker Vessels, are euer thrust to the wall: therefore I will push *Mountagues* men from the wall, and thrust his Maides to the wall. (their men.
Greg. The Quarrell is betweene our Masters, and vs
Samp. 'Tis all one, I will shew my selfe a tyrant: when I haue fought with the men, I will bee ciuill with the Maids, and cut off their heads.
Greg. The heads of the Maids?
Sam. I, the heads of the Maids, or their Maiden-heads, Take it in what sence thou wilt.
Greg. They must take it sence, that feele it.
Samp. Me they shall feele while I am able to stand: And 'tis knowne I am a pretty peece of flesh.
Greg. 'Tis well thou art not Fish: If thou had'st, thou had'st beene poore Iohn. Draw thy Toole, here comes of the House of the *Mountagues*.

Enter two other Seruingmen.

Sam. My naked weapon is out: quarrel, I wil back thee
Gre. How? Turne thy backe, and run.
Sam. Feare me not.
Gre. No marry: I feare thee.
Sam. Let vs take the Law of our sides: let them begin.
Gr. I wil frown as I passe by, & let them take it as they list
Sam. Nay, as they dare. I wil bite my Thumb at them, which is a disgrace to them, if they beare it.
Abra. Do you bite your Thumbe at vs sir?
Samp. I do bite my Thumbe, sir.
Abra. Do you bite your Thumb at vs, sir?
Sam. Is the Law of our side, if I say I? *Gre.* No.

Sam. No sir, I do not bite my Thumbe at you sir: but I bite my Thumbe sir.
Greg. Do you quarrell sir?
Abra. Quarrell sir? no sir: (as you
Sam. If you do sir, I am for you, I serue as good a man
Abra. No better? *Samp.* Well sir.

Enter Benuolio.

Gr. Say better: here comes one of my masters kinsmen.
Samp. Yes, better.
Abra. You Lye.
Samp. Draw if you be men. *Gregory*, remember thy washing blow. *They Fight.*
Ben. Part Fooles, put vp your Swords, you know not what you do.

Enter Tibalt.

Tyb. What art thou drawne, among these heartlesse Hindes? Turne thee *Benuolio*, looke vpon thy death.
Ben. I do but keepe the peace, put vp thy Sword, Or manage it to part these men with me.
Tyb. What draw, and talke of peace? I hate the word As I hate hell, all *Mountagues*, and thee: Haue at thee Coward. *Fight.*

Enter three or foure Citizens with Clubs.

Offi. Clubs, Bils, and Partisons, strike, beat them down Downe with the *Capulets*, downe with the *Mountagues*.

Enter old Capulet in his Gowne, and his wife.

Cap. What noise is this? Giue me my long Sword ho.
Wife. A crutch, a crutch: why call you for a Sword?
Cap. My Sword I say: Old *Mountague* is come, And flourishes his Blade in spight of me.

Enter old Mountague, & his wife.

Moun. Thou villaine *Capulet*. Hold me not, let me go
2 Wife. Thou shalt not stir a foote to seeke a Foe.

Enter Prince Eskales, with his Traine.

Prince. Rebellious Subiects, Enemies to peace, Prophaners of this Neighbor-stained Steele, Will they not heare? What hoe, you Men, you Beasts, That quench the fire of your pernitious Rage, With purple Fountaines issuing from your Veines: On paine of Torture, from those bloody hands Throw your mistemper'd Weapons to the ground, And heare the Sentence of your mooued Prince. Three ciuill Broyles, bred of an Ayery word, By thee old *Capulet* and *Mountague*, Haue thrice disturb'd the quiet of our streets, And made *Verona*'s ancient Citizens Cast by their Graue beseeming Ornaments, To wield old Partizans, in hands as old,

ee 3 Cankred

First page of *Romeo and Juliet* from the First Folio, 1623

A performance at the Globe Theatre

Scholars are divided as to when the play was actually written. Some place the composition date as early as 1591, and others as late as 1596.

Shakespeare's Verse and Prose

Many students find Shakespeare difficult to read and understand. They often ask whether or not the Elizabethans really spoke the way Shakespeare's characters do. The answer is, of course, no. Shakespeare wrote using a poetic form known as *blank verse*. This produces an elevated style of speech that would have been very different from everyday speech during the Elizabethan period.

Furthermore, the blank verse contains a rhythm pattern known as *iambic pentameter*. What this means is that most lines contain five feet (pentameter) and each foot contains an unstressed and a stressed syllable (an iamb). In other words, as Shakespeare wrote, playing in the back of his mind was a rhythm pattern that would sound like:

da DA da DA da DA da DA da DA

Romeo's first line in the famous balcony scene would look like this in terms of stressed and unstressed syllables:

~ / ~ / ~ / ~ / ~ /
But soft! What light through yonder window breaks.

Romeo and Juliet is approximately 3000 lines long, and of these, 370 are written in prose. Prose contrasts strongly with the elevated style of blank verse. In the play, prose is used in letters and other documents, in scenes involving servants and members of the lower classes, and in scenes of comic relief.

The Text and Stage Directions

The edition for this text is faithful to the 1599 Second Quarto. Spelling and punctuation have been modernized to make the reading more accessible to today's readers.

Shakespeare used stage directions very sparingly in his plays. Because he was directly involved in the production of the plays, there was little need for him to record the stage directions. The First Quarto of *Romeo and Juliet* includes many stage directions that do not appear in the more authoritative version. Several of these directions are included in this edition as they provide insight into how the play was first performed.

In this edition, the stage directions that appear in italics are Shakespeare's. Directions that are included in square brackets [ ] have been added by the editor. A long dash "—" in a speech indicates that the speaker is addressing someone other than the person to whom the actor was first speaking.

The following stage directions appear frequently in Shakespeare's plays:

Above, aloft – scene played in the balcony above the stage level or from higher up in the loft

Alarum – a loud shout, a signal call to arms

Aside – spoken directly to the audience and not heard by the others on the stage

Below, beneath – speech or scene played from below the surface of the stage, the actor stands inside an open trap-door

Draws – actor pulls out a sword or dagger

Exit – he/she leaves the stage

Exeunt – they leave the stage

Falls – actor is wounded and falls to the ground

Flourish – fanfare of trumpets; usually announcing the entrance of royalty

Hautboys – musicians enter, playing wind instruments

Omnes – all; everyone

Torchbearers – actors carry torches, a clue to the audience that the scene takes place in the dark, either at night or in an area that is not naturally lit

Within – words spoken off-stage in what the audience would assume is an unseen room, corridor, or the outdoors

Verona

Mantua

ITALY

Adriatic Sea

Rome

Tyrrhenian Sea

Ionian Sea

The setting for
ROMEO AND JULIET

Dramatis Personae

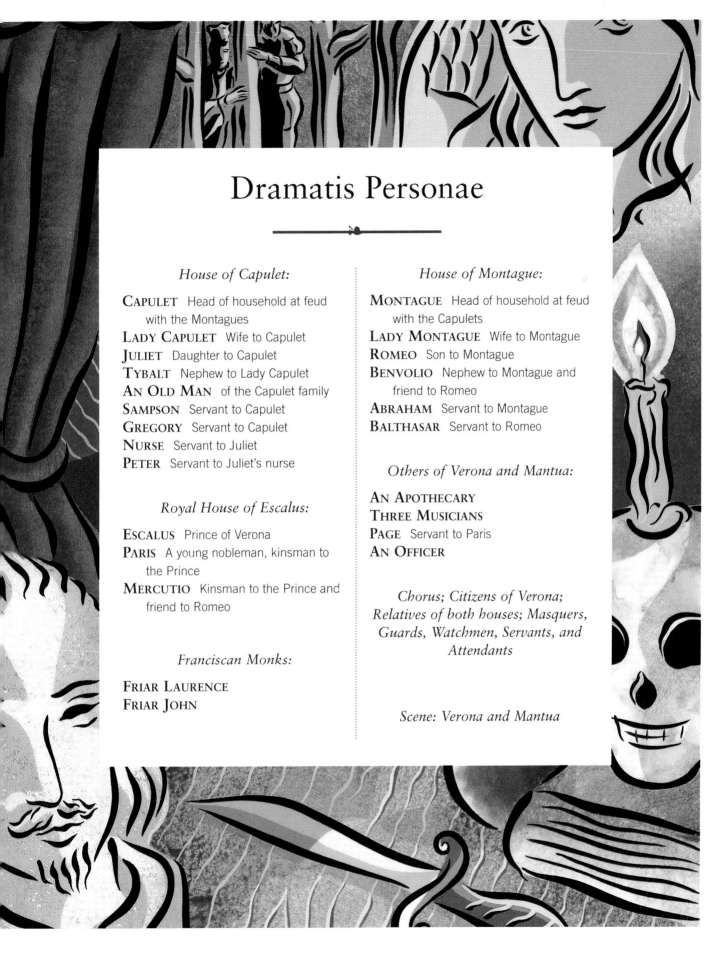

House of Capulet:

CAPULET Head of household at feud with the Montagues

LADY CAPULET Wife to Capulet

JULIET Daughter to Capulet

TYBALT Nephew to Lady Capulet

AN OLD MAN of the Capulet family

SAMPSON Servant to Capulet

GREGORY Servant to Capulet

NURSE Servant to Juliet

PETER Servant to Juliet's nurse

Royal House of Escalus:

ESCALUS Prince of Verona

PARIS A young nobleman, kinsman to the Prince

MERCUTIO Kinsman to the Prince and friend to Romeo

Franciscan Monks:

FRIAR LAURENCE

FRIAR JOHN

House of Montague:

MONTAGUE Head of household at feud with the Capulets

LADY MONTAGUE Wife to Montague

ROMEO Son to Montague

BENVOLIO Nephew to Montague and friend to Romeo

ABRAHAM Servant to Montague

BALTHASAR Servant to Romeo

Others of Verona and Mantua:

AN APOTHECARY

THREE MUSICIANS

PAGE Servant to Paris

AN OFFICER

Chorus; Citizens of Verona; Relatives of both houses; Masquers, Guards, Watchmen, Servants, and Attendants

Scene: Verona and Mantua

The Prologue

Enter Chorus.

CHORUS: Two households, both alike in dignity,
  (In fair Verona, where we lay our scene)
  From ancient grudge, break to new mutiny,
  Where civil blood makes civil hands unclean.
  From forth the fatal loins of these two foes,
  A pair of star-crossed lovers take their life,
  Whose misadventured piteous overthrows
  Doth with their death bury their parents' strife.
  The fearful passage of their death-marked love,
  And the continuance of their parents' rage,   10
  Which, but their children's end, naught could remove,
  Is now the two hours' traffic of our stage;
  The which if you with patient ears attend,
  What here shall miss, our toil shall strive to mend.

Exit.

"Two households, both alike in dignity"

This introduction to the play, spoken by the Chorus directly to the audience, is written in the form of a sonnet. In fourteen lines, the essence of the plot is revealed. The tragedy, we are told, will involve a pair of ill-fated lovers who by their deaths will end the long and bitter feud that has been raging between their families.

1. *dignity* – nobility
3. *mutiny* – violence
5. *From forth* – bred from
6. *star-crossed* – ill-fated. The Elizabethans believed that a person's destiny and character were, to a degree, determined by the stars.
7. *overthrows* – downfalls; death
11. *naught* – nothing

12. *two hours' traffic* – Is this just a convenient round number or evidence that, when plays were performed at the Globe, they were edited to fit into a two-hour performance?

RELATED READING

The Argument from Romeus and Juliet – poem by Arthur Brooke (page 135)

Act One

Scene 1

Verona. A public place.

It is early Sunday morning. Servants of two feuding families confront each other, and a street fight ensues. Prince Escalus puts an end to the brawl and declares that any further violation of the peace will be punishable by death. Romeo, meanwhile, has been spending much of his time alone. When his friend Benvolio attempts to discover the cause of his unhappiness, Romeo admits that he is in love, but that she will not return his love.

Stage Direction: *bucklers –* small round shields

buckler

1. *carry coals* – tolerate insults. Coal carriers in Shakespeare's day were held in very low esteem.
2. *colliers* – carriers of coal
3. *choler* – anger
4. *collar* – hangman's noose
8. *stand* – stay and defend one's ground

Enter Sampson and Gregory, of the house of Capulet, with swords and bucklers.

SAMPSON: Gregory, on my word, we'll not carry coals.

GREGORY: No, for then we should be colliers.

SAMPSON: I mean, if we be in choler, we'll draw.

GREGORY: Ay, while you live, draw your neck out of collar.

SAMPSON: I strike quickly being moved.

GREGORY: But thou art not quickly moved to strike.

SAMPSON: A dog of the house of Montague moves me.

GREGORY: To move is to stir, and to be valiant is to stand. Therefore, if thou art moved, thou runnest away.

SAMPSON: A dog of that house shall move me to stand. 10 I will take the wall of any man or maid of Montague's.

GREGORY: That shows thee a weak slave, for the weakest goes to the wall.

SAMPSON: 'Tis true, and therefore women, being the weaker vessels, are ever thrust to the wall. Therefore I will push Montague's men from the wall and thrust his maids to the wall.

GREGORY: The quarrel is between our masters and us their men.

SAMPSON: 'Tis all one. I will show myself a tyrant. When I have fought with the men, I will be civil with the maids; I will cut off their heads. 20

GREGORY: The heads of the maids?

SAMPSON: Ay, the heads of the maids, or their maidenheads. Take it in what sense thou wilt.

GREGORY: They must take it in sense that feel it.

SAMPSON: Me they shall feel while I am able to stand, and 'tis known I am a pretty piece of flesh.

GREGORY: 'Tis well thou art not fish. If thou hadst, thou hadst been Poor-John. Draw thy tool! Here comes of the house of Montagues.

Enter two other Servingmen, Abraham and Balthasar.

SAMPSON: My naked weapon is out. Quarrel, I will back thee.
GREGORY: How, turn thy back and run?   30
SAMPSON: Fear me not.
GREGORY: No, marry. I fear thee!
SAMPSON: Let us take the law of our sides. Let them begin.
GREGORY: I will frown as I pass by, and let them take it as they list.
SAMPSON: Nay, as they dare. I will bite my thumb at them, which is disgrace to them, if they bear it.
ABRAHAM: Do you bite your thumb at us, sir?
SAMPSON: I do bite my thumb, sir.
ABRAHAM: Do you bite your thumb at us, sir?
SAMPSON: *[Aside to Gregory.]* Is the law of our side if I say ay?   40
GREGORY: *[Aside to Sampson.]* No.
SAMPSON: No, sir, I do not bite my thumb at you, sir, but I bite my thumb, sir.
GREGORY: Do you quarrel, sir?
ABRAHAM: Quarrel, sir? No, sir.
SAMPSON: But if you do, sir, I am for you. I serve as good a man as you.
ABRAHAM: No better.
SAMPSON: Well, sir.

Enter Benvolio.

GREGORY: *[Aside to Sampson.]* Say "better." Here comes one of my master's kinsmen.   50
SAMPSON: Yes, better, sir.
ABRAHAM: You lie.
SAMPSON: Draw, if you be men. Gregory, remember thy swashing blow.

They fight.

BENVOLIO: Part, fools! Put up your swords.
    You know not what you do.

Enter Tybalt.

11. *take the wall* – Because of the Elizabethans' habit of throwing garbage out their windows and onto the streets, the sheltered walkways closest to the walls of buildings were the least foul areas to walk in. "To take the wall," or walk closest to the wall, was a sign of superiority and strength.

12 – 13. *weakest ... wall* – In street disturbances involving large numbers of people, the weakest were often pushed aside, closest to the wall.

27. *Poor-John* – dried salted fish; a poor person's meal
33. Sampson suggests that to protect themselves from punishment, they make it appear that the Montagues started the quarrel.
34. *list* – please
35. *bite my thumb* – an insulting gesture of defiance
53. *swashing* – smashing

Act One • Scene 1

56. *heartless hinds* – Two meanings are possible: a) cowardly servants, and b) female deer without a hart (male deer) to protect them.

TYBALT: What, art thou drawn among these heartless hinds?
    Turn thee Benvolio! Look upon thy death.
BENVOLIO: I do but keep the peace. Put up thy sword,
    Or manage it to part these men with me.
TYBALT: What, drawn, and talk of peace? I hate the word   60
    As I hate hell, all Montagues, and thee.
    Have at thee, coward!

They fight.
Enter an officer, and three or four Citizens
with clubs or partisans.

CITIZENS: Clubs, bills and partisans! Strike! Beat them down!
    Down with the Capulets! Down with the Montagues!

Enter old Capulet in his gown, and Lady Capulet.

63. *bills and partisans* – long-handled weapons. A partisan is a spear with a broad head.

CAPULET: What noise is this? Give me my long sword, ho!
LADY CAPULET: A crutch, a crutch! Why call you for a sword?
CAPULET: My sword, I say! Old Montague is come
    And flourishes his blade in spite of me.

Enter old Montague and Lady Montague.

MONTAGUE: Thou villain Capulet! Hold me not! Let me go!
LADY MONTAGUE: Thou shalt not stir one foot to seek a foe.   70

Enter Prince Escalus, with his Train.

partisan

72. *Profaners ... steel* – "You have disgracefully used your steel swords to shed each other's blood"
77. *mistempered* – badly tempered, or being used for an ill purpose
78. *moved* – angry
79. *bred ... word* – caused by some trivial remark
83. *Cast ... ornaments* – put aside their dignified clothing that is more suited to them
85. *Cankered ... cankered* – rusted ... malignant

PRINCE: Rebellious subjects, enemies to peace,
    Profaners of this neighbour-stained steel —
    Will they not hear? What, ho! You men, you beasts,
    That quench the fire of your pernicious rage
    With purple fountains issuing from your veins,
    On pain of torture, from those bloody hands
    Throw your mistempered weapons to the ground
    And hear the sentence of your moved prince.
    Three civil brawls, bred of an airy word
    By thee, old Capulet, and Montague,   80
    Have thrice disturbed the quiet of our streets
    And made Verona's ancient citizens
    Cast by their grave beseeming ornaments
    To wield old partisans, in hands as old,
    Cankered with peace, to part your cankered hate.
    If ever you disturb our streets again

Your lives shall pay the forfeit of the peace.
For this time all the rest depart away.
You, Capulet, shall go along with me,
And, Montague, come you this afternoon,   90
To know our farther pleasure in this case,
To old Freetown, our common judgment place.   92. *common* – public
Once more, on pain of death, all men depart.

Exeunt [all but Montague, Lady Montague, and Benvolio].

MONTAGUE: Who set this ancient quarrel new abroach?   94. *abroach* – To abroach is
    Speak, nephew, were you by when it began?   to pierce a barrel (of liquor)
BENVOLIO: Here were the servants of your adversary   and let the contents flow out.
    And yours, close fighting ere I did approach.   97. *ere* – before
    I drew to part them. In the instant came
    The fiery Tybalt, with his sword prepared,
    Which, as he breathed defiance to my ears,   100   111. *sycamore* – tree often
    He swung about his head and cut the winds,   associated with love-sickness.
    Who, nothing hurt withal, hissed him in scorn.   Could Shakespeare have also
    While we were interchanging thrusts and blows,   intended this to be an
    Came more and more, and fought on part and part,   obvious pun?
    Till the Prince came, who parted either part.   112. *rooteth* – has its roots
LADY MONTAGUE: O, where is Romeo? Saw you him today?   (referring to the grove of
    Right glad I am he was not at this fray.   trees)
BENVOLIO: Madam, an hour before the worshipped sun   114. *ware* – aware
    Peered forth the golden window of the east,   115. *covert* – shelter
    A troubled mind drove me to walk abroad,   110   116. *affections* – desires
    Where, underneath the grove of sycamore   117 – 20. *Which ... me* –
    That westward rooteth from this city's side,   Benvolio, realizing that like
    So early walking did I see your son.   himself Romeo wanted to be
    Towards him I made, but he was ware of me   alone, and feeling that even
    And stole into the covert of the wood.   his own company was too
    I, measuring his affections by my own,   much to bear, attained his
    Which then most sought where most might not be found,   desire by shunning Romeo,
    Being one too many by my weary self,   who was more than happy
    Pursued my humour, not pursuing his,   not to have any company.
    And gladly shunned who gladly fled from me.   120
MONTAGUE: Many a morning hath he there been seen,
    With tears augmenting the fresh morning's dew,   122. *augmenting* – adding to
    Adding to clouds more clouds with his deep sighs.   126. *Aurora* – goddess of the
    But all so soon as the all-cheering sun   dawn
    Should in the farthest east begin to draw   127. *heavy* – pensive,
    The shady curtains from Aurora's bed,   sorrowful; contrasted with
    Away from light steals home my heavy son   "light" in the same line
    And private in his chamber pens himself,

Shuts up his windows, locks fair daylight out
And makes himself an artificial night. 130
Black and portentous must this humour prove
Unless good counsel may the cause remove.

BENVOLIO: My noble uncle, do you know the cause?
MONTAGUE: I neither know it nor can learn of him.
BENVOLIO: Have you importuned him by any means?
MONTAGUE: Both by myself and many other friends.
But he, his own affections' counsellor,
Is to himself — I will not say how true —
But to himself so secret and so close,
So far from sounding and discovery, 140
As is the bud bit with an envious worm
Ere he can spread his sweet leaves to the air
Or dedicate his beauty to the sun.
Could we but learn from whence his sorrows grow,
We would as willingly give cure as know.

Enter Romeo.

BENVOLIO: See, where he comes. So please you step aside,
I'll know his grievance, or be much denied.
MONTAGUE: I would thou wert so happy by thy stay
To hear true shrift. Come, madam, let's away.

Exeunt [Montague and Lady Montague].

BENVOLIO: Good morrow, cousin. 150
ROMEO: Is the day so young?
BENVOLIO: But new struck nine.
ROMEO: Ay me, sad hours seem long.
Was that my father that went hence so fast?
BENVOLIO: It was. What sadness lengthens Romeo's hours?
ROMEO: Not having that which having makes them short.
BENVOLIO: In love?
ROMEO: Out.
BENVOLIO: Of love?
ROMEO: Out of her favour where I am in love. 160
BENVOLIO: Alas that love so gentle in his view
Should be so tyrannous and rough in proof.
ROMEO: Alas that love, whose view is muffled still,
Should without eyes see pathways to his will!
Where shall we dine? O me! What fray was here?
Yet tell me not, for I have heard it all.
Here's much to do with hate, but more with love.

131. *humour* – mood

135. *importuned him* – urged him to talk and reveal the cause of his depression

140. *sounding ... worm* – Sounding is a nautical term for measuring depth. In other words, the depth of Romeo's problem is as difficult to measure as finding a worm in a tiny bud.

147. *grievance* – cause of his trouble
149. *shrift* – confession

161. *love* – Cupid
161. *view* – appearance
162. *in proof* – in actual experience
163. *muffled* – covered, blindfolded
164. *pathways ... will* – means to accomplish his desires

Why then, O brawling love, O loving hate!
O anything, of nothing first create!
O heavy lightness, serious vanity,   170
Misshapen chaos of well-seeming forms!
Feather of lead, bright smoke, cold fire, sick health,
Still-waking sleep that is not what it is.
This love feel I, that feel no love in this.
Dost thou not laugh?

BENVOLIO: No, coz, I rather weep.

ROMEO: Good heart, at what?

BENVOLIO: At thy good heart's oppression.

ROMEO: Why, such is love's transgression.
Griefs of mine own lie heavy in my breast,   180
Which thou wilt propagate, to have it pressed
With more of thine. This love that thou hast shown
Doth add more grief to too much of mine own.
Love is a smoke made with the fume of sighs;
Being purged, a fire sparkling in lovers' eyes;
Being vexed, a sea nourished with lovers' tears.
What is it else? A madness most discreet,
A choking gall, and a preserving sweet.
Farewell, my coz.

BENVOLIO: Soft, I will go along.   190
And if you leave me so, you do me wrong.

ROMEO: Tut, I have lost myself, I am not here.
This is not Romeo, he's some other where.

BENVOLIO: Tell me in sadness, who is that you love?

ROMEO: What, shall I groan and tell thee?

BENVOLIO: Groan? Why, no, but sadly tell me who.

ROMEO: Bid a sick man in sadness make his will?
A word ill urged to one that is so ill.
In sadness, cousin, I do love a woman.

BENVOLIO: I aimed so near when I supposed you loved.   200

ROMEO: A right good markman, and she's fair I love.

BENVOLIO: A right fair mark, fair coz, is soonest hit.

ROMEO: Well, in that hit you miss. She'll not be hit
With Cupid's arrow. She hath Dian's wit,
And, in strong proof of chastity well armed,
From Love's weak childish bow she lives uncharmed.
She will not stay the siege of loving terms,
Nor bide the encounter of assailing eyes
Nor ope her lap to saint-seducing gold.
O, she is rich in beauty, only poor   210
That, when she dies, with beauty dies her store.

BENVOLIO: Then she hath sworn that she will still live chaste?

---

170. *O heavy lightness* – Romeo expresses his unhappiness and confusion through a series of contrasting images better known as *oxymorons*. This device works by combining two words that are opposite in meaning. "Jumbo shrimp" is one modern example of an oxymoron. The use of oxymorons serves to startle the reader and to convey how it feels to have mixed emotions. Oxymoron, incidentally, is made up of two Greek words that mean sharp and dull.

179. *transgression* – sin, way of doing wrong
181. *propagate* – increase
181. *pressed* – burdened
185. *purged* – cleared away, i.e., the smoke
186. *vexed* – crossed
187. *madness ... discreet* – a wise insanity, another oxymoron
188. *gall* – bitterness

204. *Dian's wit* – the wisdom of Diana, the Roman goddess of hunting and chastity. It appears that Romeo's love has decided to have nothing whatsoever to do with men.
207. *stay the siege* – endure the assault
211. *store* – wealth that cannot be passed on (because she intends to have no children)

Act One • Scene 1

225. *in question more* – by comparison
226. *happy masks* – In Shakespeare's day, ladies often wore black half-masks when they appeared in public.
230. *passing fair* – extremely beautiful
231 – 32. *What ... fair* – When Romeo sees an extremely beautiful girl, she serves but to remind him of one who exceeds her in beauty.
234. *I'll ... debt* – I'll convince you that my teaching is correct or die trying.

Love is all in fire, and yet
   is ever freezing,
Love is ever sick, yet is
   never dying;
Love is ever true, yet is
   ever lying;
Love does dote in liking,
   yet is mad in loathing;
Love indeed is anything;
   yet indeed is nothing.

– Thomas Middleton
(c. 1570 – 1627),
Elizabethan poet and
dramatist

ROMEO: She hath, and in that sparing makes huge waste.
   For beauty, starved with her severity,
   Cuts beauty off from all posterity.
   She is too fair, too wise, wisely too fair,
   To merit bliss by making me despair.
   She hath forsworn to love, and in that vow
   Do I live dead, that live to tell it now.
BENVOLIO: Be ruled by me, forget to think of her.   220
ROMEO: O, teach me how I should forget to think.
BENVOLIO: By giving liberty unto thine eyes.
   Examine other beauties.
ROMEO: 'Tis the way
   To call hers, exquisite, in question more.
   These happy masks that kiss fair ladies' brows,
   Being black puts us in mind they hide the fair.
   He that is strucken blind cannot forget
   The precious treasure of his eyesight lost.
   Show me a mistress that is passing fair,   230
   What doth her beauty serve but as a note
   Where I may read who passed that passing fair?
   Farewell. Thou canst not teach me to forget.
BENVOLIO: I'll pay that doctrine, or else die in debt.

Exeunt.

Act One
Scene 2

A street.

It is later in the day. Count Paris seeks permission to marry Juliet. Capulet maintains that his daughter is too young, but suggests that Paris seek her consent. Romeo and Benvolio discover that Rosaline will be invited to a ball at Capulet's house that evening, and Benvolio convinces Romeo to attend.

Enter Capulet, County Paris, and Servant the Clown.

CAPULET: But Montague is bound as well as I,
    In penalty alike, and 'tis not hard, I think,
    For men so old as we to keep the peace.
PARIS: Of honourable reckoning are you both,
    And pity 'tis you lived at odds so long.
    But now, my lord, what say you to my suit?
CAPULET: But saying over what I have said before:
    My child is yet a stranger in the world,
    She hath not seen the change of fourteen years.
    Let two more summers wither in their pride   10
    Ere we may think her ripe to be a bride.
PARIS: Younger than she are happy mothers made.
CAPULET: And too soon marred are those so early made.
    Earth hath swallowed all my hopes but she.
    She is the hopeful lady of my earth.
    But woo her, gentle Paris, get her heart;
    My will to her consent is but a part.
    And she agree, within her scope of choice
    Lies my consent and fair according voice.
    This night I hold an old accustomed feast,   20
    Whereto I have invited many a guest,
    Such as I love, and you among the store,
    One more, most welcome, makes my number more.
    At my poor house look to behold this night
    Earth-treading stars that make dark heaven light.
    Such comfort as do lusty young men feel
    When well apparelled April on the heel
    Of limping winter treads, even such delight

4. *reckoning* – reputation
6. *suit* – request

9. *fourteen years* – Fourteen was considered young for marriage, but not too young. The actual legal age of consent was twelve for girls, and fourteen for boys. It was not uncommon for noble and wealthy families to contract marriages for even younger children.

15. *hopeful … earth* – my last hope and my heir
17. "My will is less important than her consent."
18. *scope of choice* – choice that is freely hers
19. *according* – agreeing

25. *Earth-treading stars* – beautiful young ladies
26. *lusty* – vigorous, lively
27. *well apparelled* – refers to the new coat of flowers and leaves that adorns the earth

30. *Inherit* – acquire, come to possess

32 – 33. *Which ... none* – "When you see my daughter among all the other young women, she will appear to be just another person in the crowd, and may very well be not the one you would choose after all."

38. *on ... stay* – "await the pleasure of their company"

40. *yard* – tailor's measuring rod

41. *last* – model of the foot used by shoemakers to make boots

last

41. *pencil* – paintbrush

45. *learned* – those who can read

45. *In good time* – "Here comes help just when I need it."

46 – 51. Benvolio urges Romeo to remedy his situation by seeking out a new love.

48. *holp* – helped

52. *plantain leaf* – common remedy for bruises. This broad flat leaf was also used to bind wounds. Benvolio is being mocked here for oversimplifying Romeo's problem.

56 – 58. Romeo's speech provides us with a suggestion of how lunatics were treated during the Elizabethan period.

64. *Ye ... merry* – The servant misunderstands Romeo and bids him farewell.

Among fresh female buds shall you this night
Inherit at my house. Hear all, all see,   30
And like her most whose merit most shall be;
Which, on more view of many, mine, being one,
May stand in number, though in reckoning none.
Come, go with me.
     [To Servant, giving him a paper.]
      Go, sirrah, trudge about
Through fair Verona, find those persons out
Whose names are written there, and to them say,
My house and welcome on their pleasure stay.

Exeunt [Capulet and Paris].

SERVANT: Find them out whose names are written. Here it is
  written that the shoemaker should meddle with his yard 40
  and the tailor with his last, the fisher with his pencil and
  the painter with his nets, but I am sent to find those
  persons whose names are here writ, and can never find
  what names the writing person hath here writ. I must to
  the learned. In good time.

Enter Benvolio and Romeo.

BENVOLIO: Tut, man, one fire burns out another's burning,
  One pain is lessened by another's anguish.
  Turn giddy, and be holp by backward turning.
  One desperate grief cures with another's languish.
  Take thou some new infection to thy eye   50
  And the rank poison of the old will die.
ROMEO: Your plantain leaf is excellent for that.
BENVOLIO: For what, I pray thee?
ROMEO: For your broken shin.
BENVOLIO: Why, Romeo, art thou mad?
ROMEO: Not mad, but bound more than a madman is.
  Shut up in prison, kept without my food,
  Whipped and tormented and — good-even, good fellow.
SERVANT: God give good-even. I pray, sir, can you read?
ROMEO: Ay, mine own fortune in my misery.   60
SERVANT: Perhaps you have learned it without book.
  But I pray, can you read anything you see?
ROMEO: Ay, if I know the letters and the language.
SERVANT: Ye say honestly. Rest you merry!
ROMEO: Stay, fellow, I can read.

He reads the letter.

> "Signior Martino and his wife and daughters;
> County Anselme and his beauteous sisters;
> The lady widow of Utruvio;
> Signior Placentio and his lovely nieces;
> Mercutio and his brother Valentine;   70
> Mine uncle Capulet, his wife, and daughters;
> My fair niece Rosaline and Livia;
> Signior Valentio and his cousin Tybalt;
> Lucio and the lively Helena."

A fair assembly. Whither should they come?

SERVANT: Up.

ROMEO: Whither to supper?

SERVANT: To our house.

ROMEO: Whose house?

SERVANT: My master's.   80

ROMEO: Indeed I should have asked you that before.

SERVANT: Now I'll tell you without asking. My master is the great rich Capulet, and if you be not of the house of Montagues, I pray come and crush a cup of wine. Rest you merry!

Exit.

BENVOLIO: At this same ancient feast of Capulet's
Sups the fair Rosaline whom thou so loves,
With all the admired beauties of Verona.
Go thither, and with unattainted eye
Compare her face with some that I shall show,   90
And I will make thee think thy swan a crow.

ROMEO: When the devout religion of mine eye
Maintains such falsehood, then turn tears to fires;
And these who, often drowned, could never die,
Transparent heretics, be burnt for liars.
One fairer than my love? The all-seeing sun
Never saw her match since first the world begun.

BENVOLIO: Tut, you saw her fair, none else being by,
Herself poised with herself in either eye.
But in that crystal scales let there be weighed   100
Your lady's love against some other maid
That I will show you shining at this feast,
And she shall scant show well that now seems best.

ROMEO: I'll go along, no such sight to be shown,
But to rejoice in splendour of mine own.

Exeunt.

67. *County* – Count

84. *crush* – quaff, drink
86. *ancient* – established by tradition
89. *unattainted* – not infected or prejudiced (with love for Rosaline)
92 – 93. "When my eyes, which are devout in their worship (of Rosaline), accept the lie that Rosaline is not the fairest of females, let my tears turn to fire."

94 – 95. A possible reference to the sixteenth-century custom of testing heretics, or those allegedly in league with the Devil. Suspects were tied to chairs and dunked into a river. If they appeared to be drowning or if they drowned, this proved their innocence. If they floated, this was taken as evidence that supernatural forces were assisting them, and they were then burned at the stake. Romeo claims that his eyes have often drowned in tears but he does not die. His is therefore a true love.

100. *crystal scales* – Romeo's eyes are compared to a set of scales that balance the beauty of Rosaline with that of others.

Act One
Scene 3

Capulet's house.

Lady Capulet informs Juliet that Paris has asked for her hand in marriage. Juliet reveals that she has not even dreamed of marriage, but is willing to consider the proposal if this is what her parents wish.

Enter Lady Capulet and Nurse.

LADY CAPULET: Nurse, where's my daughter? Call her forth to me.
NURSE: Now, by my maidenhead at twelve year old,
    I bade her come. What, lamb! What ladybird!
    God forbid! Where's this girl? What, Juliet!

Enter Juliet.

JULIET: How now? Who calls?
NURSE: Your mother.
JULIET: Madam, l am here, what is your will?
LADY CAPULET: This is the matter. Nurse, give leave awhile,
    We must talk in secret. Nurse, come back again.
    I have remembered me, thou's hear our counsel.   10
    Thou knowest my daughter's of a pretty age.
NURSE: Faith, I can tell her age unto an hour.
LADY CAPULET: She's not fourteen.
NURSE: I'll lay fourteen of my teeth —
    And yet, to my teen be it spoken, I have but four —
    She's not fourteen. How long is it now
    To Lammas-tide?
LADY CAPULET: A fortnight and odd days.
NURSE: Even or odd, of all days in the year,
    Come Lammas Eve at night shall she be fourteen.   20
    Susan and she — God rest all Christian souls —
    Were of an age. Well, Susan is with God.
    She was too good for me. But, as I said,
    On Lammas Eve at night shall she be fourteen.
    That shall she. Marry, I remember it well.
    'Tis since the earthquake now eleven years,

10. *thou's* – thou shalt
15. *teen* – sorrow
17. *Lammas-tide* – August 1, the date of a harvest festival celebrating the first ripe corn. Lammas is an Old English word for loaves, which were made from corn.

20. This detail gives us a fairly precise date for the action of the play – two weeks or so before Juliet's fourteenth birthday. Perhaps Juliet was named for the month of her birth.

And she was weaned — I never shall forget it —
Of all the days of the year, upon that day.
For I had then laid wormwood to my dug,
Sitting in the sun under the dovehouse wall.   30
My lord and you were then at Mantua —
Nay, I do bear a brain. But, as I said,
When it did taste the wormwood on the nipple
Of my dug and felt it bitter, pretty fool,
To see it tetchy and fall out with the dug.
Shake, quoth the dovehouse! 'Twas no need, I trow,
To bid me trudge.
And since that time it is eleven years,
For then she could stand high-lone, nay, by the rood,
She could have run and waddled all about.   40
For even the day before, she broke her brow,
And then my husband — God be with his soul,
He was a merry man — took up the child.
"Yea," quoth he, "dost thou fall upon thy face?
Thou wilt fall backward when thou hast more wit,
Wilt thou not, Jule?" And, by my holidame,
The pretty wretch left crying, and said "Ay."
To see now how a jest shall come about!
I warrant, and I should live a thousand years
I never should forget it. "Wilt thou not, Jule?" quoth he,   50
And, pretty fool, it stinted, and said "Ay."

LADY CAPULET: Enough of this. I pray thee hold thy peace.

NURSE: Yes, madam. Yet I cannot choose but laugh
To think it should leave crying and say "Ay."
And yet, I warrant, it had upon its brow
A bump as big as a young cockerel's stone,
A perilous knock, and it cried bitterly.
"Yea," quoth my husband, "fallest upon thy face?
Thou wilt fall backward when thou comest to age,
Wilt thou not, Jule?" It stinted, and said "Ay."   60

JULIET: And stint thou too, I pray thee, nurse, say I.

NURSE: Peace, I have done. God mark thee to his grace,
Thou wast the prettiest babe that ever I nursed.
And I might live to see thee married once,
I have my wish.

LADY CAPULET: Marry, that "marry" is the very theme
I came to talk of. Tell me, daughter Juliet,
How stands your disposition to be married?

JULIET: It is an honour that I dream not of.

NURSE: An honour? Were not I thine only nurse,   70
I would say thou hadst sucked wisdom from thy teat.

29. *wormwood* – bitter medicinal oil
29. *dug* – breast
32. *bear a brain* – have a good memory
33. *it* – i.e., Juliet
35. *tetchy* – touchy, ill-tempered
35. *fall out* – quarrel; be irritated
36. *Shake ... dovehouse* – In other words, the dovehouse shook.
36. *trow* – am certain
37. *trudge* – leave
39. *high-lone* – unsupported, on her own
39. *rood* – Christ's cross
46. *holidame* – holiness

51. *stinted* – stopped

56. *stone* – testicle

71. The Nurse jokes by taking credit for Juliet's wisdom.

Act One • Scene 3

75. your mother – According to this line, Juliet's mother is approximately twenty-eight years old. This is inconsistent with the reference in Act Five, which suggests Lady Capulet is old. Some scholars have suggested that this line may contain an error. The typesetter may have substituted "your" for "a." In other words, Juliet may have been the last child born to the Capulets. The others, as mentioned by Capulet in the previous scene, did not survive.

79. man of wax – perfect and without flaw, as if he were made out of wax

84 – 95. Lady Capulet invites Juliet to peruse Paris as if he were a beautiful book in need of a binding and a cover. This use of an ingenious, elaborate, and extended comparison is called a *conceit*. Shakespeare is famous for his skillfully wrought conceits.

86. married lineament – features that join together in a harmonious manner

89. margent – commentary in the margins of a book

100. if ... move – if looking will move me to like

101. endart – pierce like an arrow or dart

105. in extremity – in confusion

107. stays – awaits

LADY CAPULET: Well, think of marriage now. Younger than you,
    Here in Verona, ladies of esteem,
    Are made already mothers. By my count,
    I was your mother much upon these years
    That you are now a maid. Thus then in brief:
    The valiant Paris seeks you for his love.
NURSE: A man, young lady! Lady, such a man
    As all the world — why he's a man of wax.
LADY CAPULET: Verona's summer hath not such a flower.   80
NURSE: Nay, he's a flower, in faith — a very flower.
LADY CAPULET: What say you? Can you love the gentleman?
    This night you shall behold him at our feast.
    Read over the volume of young Paris' face,
    And find delight writ there with beauty's pen.
    Examine every married lineament,
    And see how one another lends content.
    And what obscured in this fair volume lies
    Find written in the margent of his eyes,
    This precious book of love, this unbound lover,   90
    To beautify him only lacks a cover.
    The fish lives in the sea, and 'tis much pride
    For fair without the fair within to hide.
    That book in many's eyes doth share the glory,
    That in gold clasps locks in the golden story.
    So shall you share all that he doth possess,
    By having him making yourself no less.
NURSE: No less, nay, bigger! Women grow by men.
LADY CAPULET: Speak briefly, can you like of Paris' love?
JULIET: I'll look to like, if looking liking move,   100
    But no more deep will I endart mine eye
    Than your consent gives strength to make it fly.

Enter a Servingman.

SERVANT: Madam, the guests are come, supper served up, you called, my young lady asked for, the Nurse cursed in the pantry, and everything in extremity. I must hence to wait. I beseech you follow straight.

Exit Servingman.

LADY CAPULET: We follow thee. Juliet, the County stays.
NURSE: Go, girl, seek happy nights to happy days.

Exeunt.

Act One
Scene 4

A street.

Romeo and his friends are about to join the Capulets' party. When Romeo mentions that he has had a dream, Mercutio speaks at length of Queen Mab, the sower of dreams, and concludes that dreams are meaningless. Nevertheless, Romeo fears that some tragic consequence will result from the events of this evening.

*Enter Romeo, Mercutio, Benvolio,
with five or six other Masquers; Torchbearers.*

ROMEO: What, shall this speech be spoke for our excuse?
Or shall we on without apology?
BENVOLIO: The date is out of such prolixity.
We'll have no Cupid hoodwinked with a scarf,
Bearing a Tartar's painted bow of lath,
Scaring the ladies like a crowkeeper,
Nor no without-book prologue, faintly spoke
After the prompter, for our entrance.
But let them measure us by what they will,
We'll measure them a measure and be gone.   10
ROMEO: Give me a torch. I am not for this ambling.
Being but heavy, I will bear the light.
MERCUTIO: Nay, gentle Romeo, we must have you dance.
ROMEO: Not I, believe me. You have dancing shoes
With nimble soles, I have a soul of lead
So stakes me to the ground I cannot move.
MERCUTIO: You are a lover. Borrow Cupid's wings
And soar with them above a common bound.
ROMEO: I am too sore enpierced with his shaft
To soar with his light feathers, and so bound   20
I cannot bound a pitch above dull woe.
Under love's heavy burden do I sink.
MERCUTIO: And, to sink in it, should you burden love —
Too great oppression for a tender thing.
ROMEO: Is love a tender thing? It is too rough,
Too rude, too boisterous, and it pricks like thorn.

Heartbroken from Rosaline

1 – 2. "Shall we explain our uninvited presence or should we just enter without apology?"
3. "Such wordy formalities are no longer fashionable."
4. *hoodwinked* – blindfolded

Cupid hoodwinked

5. *Tartar's ... lath* – lip-shaped bow made from flimsy material; toy bow
6. *crowkeeper* – boy hired to scare off birds
4 – 10. Benvolio suggests that they need not announce their presence in an ostentatious way. They should enter, have one dance, and then leave.
12. *heavy* – i.e., heavy at heart. This line contains another pun, typical of Romeo's clever wit.
20. *bound* – pun; to be tied down, burdened, and to leap or dance
21. *pitch* – height

Act One • Scene 4

29. *case* – mask

30 – 32. Mercutio intends to cover what he considers an ugly face with an ugly mask, and he cares not what others think about his doing so.

35. *wantons* – merry-makers

36. *rushes* – Grasses and reeds were often strewn on floors, and even on the surface of the stage.

37 – 38. "I'll follow the good old-fashioned proverb that the spectator has the better view of the game, and be content to look on (while the rest of you dance and have fun)."

39. Another proverb advises the gambler to leave the game while he is still ahead.

40. *dun* – dark brown. Mercutio suggests that only the mouse should be dark and silent.

43. *burn daylight* – waste time

47 – 48. Mercutio claims that his good sense is five times better than that which can be determined by the five senses.

50. *no wit* – not wise

59. *agate* – semi-precious stone

61. *atomi* – atoms; tiny creatures

65. *traces* – harness

67. *film* – gossamer; fine fabric

MERCUTIO: If love be rough with you, be rough with love.
Prick love for pricking, and you beat love down.
Give me a case to put my visage in.
A visor for a visor! What care I   30
What curious eye doth quote deformities?
Here are the beetle brows shall blush for me.

BENVOLIO: Come, knock and enter, and no sooner in
But every man betake him to his legs.

ROMEO: A torch for me! Let wantons light of heart
Tickle the senseless rushes with their heels,
For I am proverbed with a grandsire phrase —
I'll be a candle-holder and look on.
The game was never so fair, and I am done.

MERCUTIO: Tut, dun's the mouse, the constable's own word.   40
If thou art dun, we'll draw thee from the mire
Of — save your reverence — love, wherein thou stickest
Up to the ears. Come, we burn daylight, ho!

ROMEO: Nay, that's not so.

MERCUTIO: I mean, sir, in delay
We waste our lights in vain, like lights by day.
Take our good meaning, for our judgment sits
Five times in that ere once in our five wits.

ROMEO: And we mean well, in going to this masque,
But 'tis no wit to go.   50

MERCUTIO: Why, may one ask?

ROMEO: I dreamt a dream tonight.

MERCUTIO: And so did I.

ROMEO: Well, what was yours?

MERCUTIO: That dreamers often lie.

ROMEO: In bed asleep, while they do dream things true.

MERCUTIO: O, then I see Queen Mab hath been with you.
She is the fairies' midwife, and she comes
In shape no bigger than an agate stone
On the forefinger of an alderman,   60
Drawn with a team of little atomi
Over men's noses as they lie asleep.
Her wagon spokes made of long spinners' legs,
The cover, of the wings of grasshoppers,
Her traces, of the smallest spider web,
Her collars, of the moonshine's watery beams,
Her whip, of cricket's bone, the lash of film,
Her waggoner, a small grey-coated gnat,
Not half so big as a round little worm
Pricked from the lazy finger of a maid.   70

Act One • Scene 4

Her chariot is an empty hazelnut,
Made by the joiner squirrel or old grub,
Time out of mind the fairies' coachmakers.
And in this state she gallops night by night
Through lovers' brains, and then they dream of love.
Over courtiers' knees, that dream on curtsies straight,
Over lawyers' fingers, who straight dream on fees,
Over ladies' lips, who straight on kisses dream,
Which oft the angry Mab with blisters plagues
Because their breaths with sweetmeats tainted are.   80
Sometime she gallops over a courtier's nose,
And then dreams he of smelling out a suit.
And sometime comes she with a tithe-pig's tail
Tickling a parson's nose as he lies asleep.
Then dreams he of another benefice.
Sometimes she driveth over a soldier's neck,
And then dreams he of cutting foreign throats,
Of breaches, ambuscados, Spanish blades,
Of healths five fathom deep. And then anon
Drums in his ear, at which he starts and wakes,   90
And being thus frighted, swears a prayer or two
And sleeps again. This is that very Mab
That plaits the manes of horses in the night
And bakes the elflocks in foul sluttish hairs,
Which once untangled much misfortune bodes
This is the hag, when maids lie on their backs,
That presses them and learns them first to bear,
Making them women of good carriage.
This is she —

ROMEO: Peace, peace, Mercutio, peace!   100
Thou talkest of nothing.

MERCUTIO: True, I talk of dreams,
Which are the children of an idle brain,
Begot of nothing but vain fantasy,
Which is as thin of substance as the air,
And more inconstant than the wind, who woos
Even now the frozen bosom of the North
And, being angered, puffs away from thence,
Turning his side to the dew-dropping south.

BENVOLIO: This wind you talk of blows us from ourselves.   110
Supper is done, and we shall come too late.

ROMEO: I fear, too early, for my mind misgives
Some consequence, yet hanging in the stars
Shall bitterly begin his fearful date

star-crossed lovers

---

72. *joiner* – carpenter

83. *tithe-pig's tail* – A tithe is
a contribution to the support of
the Church. People were
expected to contribute one-tenth
of their earnings or produce.
Therefore, out of a litter of ten,
one piglet was due as a tithe
payment.

85. *benefice* – living
88. *breaches, ambuscados* –
breaks made in defensive walls
by the enemy; ambushes
89. *healths* – tall drinks,
toasts
93 – 94. *plaits ... hairs* –
tangles the manes of horses.
A popular superstition held
that tangled and dirty hair was
the work of mischievous elves.

102. *I talk of dreams* – The
point of Mercutio's rambling
speech is that we dream of
things that relate to our lives.
A lover will dream of love, a
courtier of the court, and a
soldier of battle. He wishes to
convince Romeo that he should
not pay any attention to dreams.
According to Mercutio, they
mean nothing.

110. *ourselves* – our original
intention to go to the party
112. *misgives* – fears
113. *yet ... stars* – written in
the stars but not yet revealed.
This image should take us
back to the "star-crossed
lovers" mentioned in the
Prologue of the play.

112 – 119. Earlier in this scene, Romeo talked about a dream. Perhaps the premonition spoken about in this speech is a reference back to the dream. He fears the events of this evening will somehow result in an untimely death. Nevertheless, Romeo ignores the premonition and chooses to go forward. This defiance of warnings and forebodings is a common element in tragedy.

Stage Direction: Romeo and his friends do not exit. They march about and then retire to the side. The entrance of the servingmen marks the beginning of Scene 5.

On Mercutio: "Oh! How shall I describe that exquisite ebullience and overflow of youthful life?" – Samuel Taylor Coleridge (1772 – 1834), English author, Romantic poet, and critic

With this night's revels and expire the term
Of a despised life, closed in my breast,
By some vile forfeit of untimely death.
But he that hath the steerage of my course
Direct my sail! On, lusty gentlemen!
BENVOLIO: Strike, drum. 120

They march about the stage.

Mercutio
+
dreams
→ don't make sense
→ meaningless
→ NO FATE

Romeo
+
dreams
→ do have meaning
→ sad, fearful mood
→ "hanging in the stars" is an "untimely death"
→ FATE IS REAL

horoscopes → lead to destiny

* fate vs. chance

fate can determine your life

Act One

Scene 5

The same.

Servingmen come forth with napkins.

FIRST SERVANT: Where's Potpan that he helps not to take away?
He shift a trencher! He scrape a trencher!
SECOND SERVANT: When good manners shall lie all in one or
two men's hands, and they unwashed too, 'tis a foul thing.
FIRST SERVANT: Away with the joint-stools, remove the court-
cupboard, look to the plate. Good thou, save me a piece of
marchpane and as thou loves me, let the porter let in Susan
Grindstone and Nell — Anthony, and Potpan!
SECOND SERVANT: Ay, boy, ready.
FIRST SERVANT: You are looked for and called for, asked for
and sought for, in the great chamber.   10
THIRD SERVANT: We cannot be here and there too. Cheerly,
boys! Be brisk awhile, and the longer liver take all.

Exeunt [Servingmen].
Enter with Servants, Capulet, his Wife, Juliet, Tybalt,
and all the Guests and Gentlewomen to the Masquers.

CAPULET: Welcome, gentlemen! Ladies that have their toes
Unplagued with corns will walk a bout with you.
Ah, my mistresses, which of you all
Will now deny to dance? She that makes dainty,
She I'll swear hath corns. Am I come near ye now?
Welcome, gentlemen! I have seen the day
That I have worn a visor and could tell
A whispering tale in a fair lady's ear,   20
Such as would please. 'Tis gone, 'tis gone, 'tis gone.
You are welcome, gentlemen! Come, musicians, play.
A hall, a hall, give room — and foot it girls.

Several servants banter about the course of the evening. Capulet welcomes the disguised Romeo and his friends. Tybalt, recognizing Romeo, threatens to deal with the intruder immediately, but is prevented from doing so by Capulet. Romeo and Juliet meet and fall instantly in love. As the party breaks up, they each discover the other's identity.

1 – 12. This short scene among the servants serves to establish that some time has passed in the progress of the feast. They complain that they are short-staffed and that Potpan is dallying by not helping to take away the dirty wooden platters (trenchers).
7. *marchpane* – marzipan; a dessert made from eggs, almonds, and sugar
12. *longer liver* – he who lives the longest

16. *makes dainty* – hesitates

23. *A hall, a hall* – clear the floor (for dancing)

Music plays, and they dance.

More light, you knaves, and turn the tables up,
And quench the fire, the room is grown too hot.
Ah, sirrah, this unlooked-for sport comes well.
Nay, sit, nay, sit, good cousin Capulet,
For you and I are past our dancing days.
How long is it now since last yourself and I
Were in a masque?   30

SECOND CAPULET: By'r lady, thirty years.

CAPULET: What, man, 'tis not so much, 'tis not so much!
'Tis since the nuptial of Lucentio,
Come Pentecost as quickly as it will,
Some five-and-twenty years, and then we masqued.

SECOND CAPULET: 'Tis more, 'tis more! His son is elder, sir;
His son is thirty.

CAPULET: Will you tell me that?
His son was but a ward two years ago.

ROMEO: *[To a Servingman.]*
What lady's that, which doth enrich the hand   40
Of yonder knight?

SERVANT: I know not, sir.

ROMEO: O, she doth teach the torches to burn bright.
It seems she hangs upon the cheek of night
Like a rich jewel in an Ethiop's ear —
Beauty too rich for use, for earth too dear.
So shows a snowy dove trooping with crows
As yonder lady over her fellows shows.
The measure done, I'll watch her place of stand
And, touching hers, make blessed my rude hand.   50
Did my heart love till now? Forswear it, sight.
For I never saw true beauty till this night.

TYBALT: This, by his voice, should be a Montague.
Fetch me my rapier, boy. What, dares the slave
Come hither, covered with an antic face,
To fleer and scorn at our solemnity?
Now, by the stock and honour of my kin,
To strike him dead I hold it not a sin.

CAPULET: Why, how now, kinsman? Wherefore storm you so?

TYBALT: Uncle, this is a Montague, our foe.   60
A villain, that is hither come in spite
To scorn at our solemnity this night.

CAPULET: Young Romeo is it?

---

25. *quench the fire* – The play takes place during July, and surely there is no need for a fire in Italy during the hot summer months. This detail may be explained by the fact that in Brooke's ballad the feast was held near Christmas (see page 6).

30. *masque* – elaborate entertainment involving the wearing of masks

34. *Pentecost* – Whitsuntide, or the seventh Sunday after Easter

39. *ward* – a young person placed under guardianship till the age of 21

49. *measure* – dance

55. *antic face* – fantastical or grotesque mask

56. *fleer* – sneer

TYBALT: 'Tis he, that villain Romeo.

CAPULET: Content thee, gentle coz, let him alone.
He bears him like a portly gentleman,
And, to say truth, Verona brags of him
To be a virtuous and well-governed youth.
I would not for the wealth of all this town
Here in my house do him disparagement. 70
Therefore be patient, take no note of him.
It is my will, the which if thou respect,
Show a fair presence and put off these frowns,
An ill-beseeming semblance for a feast.

TYBALT: It fits when such a villain is a guest.
I'll not endure him.

CAPULET: He shall be endured.
What, goodman boy? I say he shall. Go to.
Am I the master here or you? Go to!
You'll not endure him? God shall mend my soul, 80
You'll make a mutiny among my guests,
You will set cock-a-hoop, you'll be the man!

TYBALT: Why, uncle, 'tis a shame.

CAPULET: Go to, go to!
You are a saucy boy. Is it so, indeed?
This trick may chance to scathe you. I know what.
You must contrary me! Marry, 'tis time. —
Well said, my hearts — You are a princox, go!
Be quiet, or — More light, more light! — For shame,
I'll make you quiet. What, cheerly, my hearts! 90

TYBALT: Patience perforce with wilful choler meeting
Makes my flesh tremble in their different greeting.
I will withdraw, but this intrusion shall,
Now seeming sweet, convert to bitterest gall.

Exit.

ROMEO: If I profane with my unworthiest hand
This holy shrine, the gentle sin is this:
My lips, two blushing pilgrims, ready stand
To smooth that rough touch with a tender kiss.

JULIET: Good pilgrim, you do wrong your hand too much,
Which mannerly devotion shows in this. 100
For saints have hands that pilgrims' hands do touch,
And palm to palm is holy palmers' kiss.

ROMEO: Have not saints lips, and holy palmers too?

66. *portly* – of good deportment, conduct

70. *disparagement* – an indignity

78. *goodman boy* – Below the rank of gentleman is a goodman. Capulet accuses Tybalt of being young and without manners.

82. "You would cause confusion and disorder (cock-a-hoop)? You would give the orders in my house?"

86. *scathe* – work against

88. *princox* – impertinent youth

91. *Patience ... meeting* – Tybalt is torn between his enforced patience and his seething anger (choler) at Romeo's intrusion.

95 – 109. These fourteen lines of dialogue, which mark the first meeting between Romeo and Juliet, take the form of a Shakespearean sonnet.

96. *shrine* – i.e., Juliet's hand

99. *pilgrim* – Florio's dictionary, published in 1598, defined *romeo* as a *pilgrim*, one who travels to the Holy Land. Pilgrims were known to carry palm leaves, and were therefore also known as *palmers*.

RELATED READING

Albert, the Perfect Waiter – poem by Bert Almon (page 157)

102. *palmers* – pilgrims (who bear palm leaves)

JULIET: Ay, pilgrim, lips that they must use in prayer.
ROMEO: O, then, dear saint, let lips do what hands do.
　　They pray, grant thou, lest faith turn to despair.
JULIET: Saints do not move, though grant for prayers' sake.
ROMEO: Then move not while my prayer's effect I take.

[He kisses her.]

　　Thus from my lips, by thine, my sin is purged.　　110
JULIET: Then have my lips the sin that they have took.
ROMEO: Sin from my lips? O trespass sweetly urged.
　　Give me my sin again.

[He kisses her.]

JULIET: You kiss by the book.
NURSE: Madam, your mother craves a word with you.
ROMEO: What is her mother?
NURSE: Marry, bachelor,
　　Her mother is the lady of the house,
　　And a good lady, and a wise and virtuous.
　　I nursed her daughter that you talked withal.　　120
　　I tell you, he that can lay hold of her
　　Shall have the chinks.

107. *Saints* – stone statues of saints

The play is "no more than a love song in disguise."
– George Moore (1852 – 1933), Irish novelist

114. "You kiss as though you had learned your skill from a book."

122. *chinks* – coins. The word comes from the sound made when coins are jostled or rubbed together.

ROMEO: Is she a Capulet?
    O dear account. My life is my foe's debt.
BENVOLIO: Away, be gone, the sport is at the best.
ROMEO: Ay, so I fear, the more is my unrest.
CAPULET: Nay, gentlemen, prepare not to be gone,
    We have a trifling foolish banquet towards.

They whisper in his ear.

Is it even so? Why then, I thank you all.   130
I thank you, honest gentlemen. Good night.
More torches here!

[Exeunt Masquers.]

    Come on then, let's to bed.
Ah, sirrah, by my fay, it waxes late,
I'll to my rest.

Exeunt [all but Juliet and Nurse].

JULIET: Come hither, Nurse. What is yond gentleman?
NURSE: The son and heir of old Tiberio.
JULIET: What's he that now is going out of door?

124. *dear account* – costly reckoning

129. *towards* – about to be served

134. *fay* – faith
134. *waxes* – grows

NURSE: Marry, that I think be young Petruchio.
JULIET: What's he that follows there, that would not dance?   140
NURSE: I know not.
JULIET: Go ask his name. *[Nurse leaves briefly.]*
                            If he be married,
      My grave is like to be my wedding bed.
NURSE: His name is Romeo, and a Montague,
      The only son of your great enemy.
JULIET: My only love sprung from my only hate.
      Too early seen unknown, and known too late.
      Prodigious birth of love it is to me
      That I must love a loathed enemy.
NURSE: What's this? What's this?
JULIET: A rhyme I learnt even now   150
      Of one I danced withal.

One calls within, "Juliet."

NURSE: Anon, anon!
      Come, let's away, the strangers all are gone.

Exeunt.

෨ ෨ ෨

147. "I saw him before I knew who he was, and now that I do know, it is too late not to fall in love."

In an earlier scene, Capulet invited Paris to attend this feast and begin his wooing of Juliet. Later, Juliet's mother also mentioned that Paris would be attending the event. Interestingly though, he does not appear at all during this scene. Perhaps Shakespeare purposely avoided referring to Paris's presence at the party in order to focus the audience's attention on the two lovers.

Act One Considerations

The Prologue

▶ The Prologue provides many of the most basic details of the story line. Some critics believe that too much is given away in terms of the plot. How do you feel? What purpose does this speech serve? Does the Prologue give away too much, thereby reducing the suspense? Or does the Prologue create a different kind of suspense? Explain.

ACT ONE Scene 1

▶ Although *Romeo and Juliet* is a tragedy, much of the play is quite comic. Outline briefly the comic elements in this scene. To what extent is Romeo's infatuation for Rosaline comic?

▶ The most important character introduced in the early part of this scene is Tybalt. Although he speaks only five lines, he leaves an unforgettable impression on the reader/audience. Choose one of his speeches and copy it on a blank piece of paper. Find illustrations from magazines and create a collage that you think serves to convey the kind of person that Tybalt is.

▶ Imagine that you are Romeo or Rosaline, and that you have been keeping a diary. Write a diary entry in which you express your deepest feelings about love. You may even wish to include a short poem in your diary.

▶ Is Romeo in love with Rosaline or is it infatuation? What is the difference? If you had a friend who was in a similar situation to Romeo's, what advice would you give that person? You may respond to this activity in the form of a letter, a telephone conversation, or a dialogue.

ACT ONE Scene 2

▶ It was not uncommon during Shakespeare's day for girls to marry at fourteen. How does Capulet feel about arranging a marriage for Juliet at this age? Write a dialogue between Capulet and his wife in which they discuss the issue of teenage marriage.

▶ *Romeo and Juliet* has been called a tragedy of fate because its ending depends so much on chance and coincidence. What evidence in this scene can be used to support this view? Dedicate a separate page in your notebook to this activity. As you go though the play and encounter other examples of chance or coincidence, add them to this list.

ACT ONE Scene 3

▶ This play contains a number of characters who are truly comic in their effect. The Nurse is one of them. If you were casting this play, whom would you choose to play the part of the Nurse? Why?

▶ Although Juliet does not speak very many lines in this scene, we learn a great deal about her character. What are your first impressions of Juliet?

▶ In lines 84 to 95, Lady Capulet utilizes an extended metaphor to describe Paris. She compares Paris to a book and Juliet to a cover that will make the book complete. Write a short paragraph or poem using an extended metaphor in which you compare a person to an interesting object.

ACT ONE Scene 4

▶ What two views of dreams are presented in this scene? Which do you find yourself in most agreement with? Why?

▶ We can assume that Mercutio, like Romeo, is a teenager. What are your first impressions of Mercutio? How would a friend describe Mercutio? How would a teacher describe him?

▶ The "Queen Mab" speech is considered by some critics to be an add-on. In other words, it is believed that Shakespeare already had a long poem written about Queen Mab and, therefore, included it in this play. What do you think? Does the speech serve any dramatic purpose? Write a dialogue between Shakespeare and his editor in which they discuss the importance of this speech to the scene.

▶ In his last speech of this scene, Romeo shares with his friends a premonition he has had of the night's events. Rewrite this premonition as a horoscope reading for Romeo.

▶ This scene contains a number of "dances" that occur in various parts of the stage and involve different groups of characters. To bring these "dances" to life, in groups, create a series of tableaux of important moments in this scene. A *tableau* is like a living picture in which a group of individuals arrange themselves so as to recreate a dramatic freeze-frame of a scene.

▶ Despite the events in the first scene of the play, it can be argued that the animosity between the feuding families is not as intense as Tybalt would like to believe. What evidence occurs in this scene that supports this view?

▶ Romeo and Juliet fall in love at first sight and express their love for each other, not only in religious terms, but also through the sonnet form. What effect do you think Shakespeare intended to create by depicting the lovers' meeting in this way?

▶ Why does Juliet ask the Nurse about the other guests before directing her attention to determining the identity of Romeo? What does this tactic suggest about Juliet's character?

Act Two
Prologue

This is the third sonnet to be found in this play. The Chorus states that Romeo's old desire for Rosaline has been replaced by his new love for Juliet, and that Juliet loves Romeo in return. We are also reminded of how difficult it will be for the two lovers to express their love to each other.

Enter Chorus.

CHORUS: Now old desire doth in his deathbed lie
And young affection gapes to be his heir;
That fair for which love groaned for and would die,
With tender Juliet matched, is now not fair.
Now Romeo is beloved and loves again,
Alike bewitched by the charm of looks,
But to his foe supposed he must complain,
And she steal love's sweet bait from fearful hooks.
Being held a foe, he may not have access
To breathe such vows as lovers use to swear,   10
And she as much in love, her means much less
To meet her new beloved anywhere,
But passion lends them power, time means, to meet,
Tempering extremities with extreme sweet.

Exit.

1. *old desire* – Romeo's old love for Rosaline
2. *young affection* – Romeo's new love for Juliet
2. *gapes* – longs hungrily, as with an open mouth
3. *fair* – i.e., Rosaline
6. *Alike* – both
7. *foe* – Juliet, because she is a Capulet

14. "Softening hardships with extreme joy."

Outside the wall of Capulet's orchard, Romeo hides and overhears his friends joke about him. Mercutio and Benvolio are obviously under the impression that Romeo is still in love with Rosaline.

2. *dull earth* – Romeo reprimands himself as being slow (dull) and base for not moving towards the centre of his universe – Juliet.

8. *conjure* – call forth not only the body but also the spirit. It was believed that one could conjure up a spirit by correctly naming it.

9. *Humours* – moody
13. *gossip* – close associate
13. *Venus* – goddess of love
14. *purblind* – totally blind
15. *Abraham* – a nickname for beggars who pretended to be insane and went around (like Cupid) half-naked

15 – 16. In an old ballad we hear of the power of Cupid in causing King Cophetua to fall in love with a beggar maid.

18. *ape* – a possible reference to a magic trick in which an ape plays dead until it is brought back to life through the conjuring of its master
22. *demesnes* – domains, areas

Act Two
Scene 1

A lane by the wall of Capulet's orchard.

Enter Romeo alone.

ROMEO: Can I go forward when my heart is here?
Turn back, dull earth, and find thy centre out.

[He climbs the wall and leaps down within it.]
Enter Benvolio with Mercutio.

BENVOLIO: Romeo! My cousin Romeo! Romeo!
MERCUTIO: He is wise,
And on my life hath stolen him home to bed.
BENVOLIO: He ran this way and leapt this orchard wall.
Call, good Mercutio.
MERCUTIO: Nay, I'll conjure too.
Romeo! Humours! Madman! Passion! Lover!
Appear thou in the likeness of a sigh,   10
Speak but one rhyme, and I am satisfied.
Cry but "Ay me!" pronounce but "love" and "dove,"
Speak to my gossip Venus one fair word,
One nickname for her purblind son and heir,
Young Abraham Cupid, he that shot so trim
When King Cophetua loved the beggar maid.
He heareth not, he stirreth not, he moveth not.
The ape is dead and I must conjure him.
I conjure thee by Rosaline's bright eyes.
By her high forehead and her scarlet lip,   20
By her fine foot, straight leg, and quivering thigh,
And the demesnes that there adjacent lie,
That in thy likeness thou appear to us!

BENVOLIO: And if he hear thee, thou wilt anger him.

MERCUTIO: This cannot anger him. 'Twould anger him
    To raise a spirit in his mistress' circle
    Of some strange nature, letting it there stand
    Till she had laid it and conjured it down.
    That were some spite. My invocation
    Is fair and honest. In his mistress' name,   30
    I conjure only but to raise up him.

BENVOLIO: Come, he hath hid himself among these trees
    To be consorted with the humorous night.
    Blind is his love and best befits the dark.

MERCUTIO: If love be blind, love cannot hit the mark.
    Now will he sit under a medlar tree
    And wish his mistress were that kind of fruit
    As maids call medlars when they laugh alone.
    O, Romeo, that she were, O that she were
    An open *et cetera*, thou a poperin pear!   40
    Romeo, good night. I'll to my truckle-bed.
    This field-bed is too cold for me to sleep.
    Come, shall we go?

BENVOLIO: Go then, for 'tis in vain
    To seek him here that means not to be found.

Exeunt.

33. *consorted* – associated
33. *humorous* – damp, moody
36. *medlar* – a tree whose small, apple-shaped fruit is not ready until it is almost rotten

medlar

41. *truckle-bed* – small comfortable bed

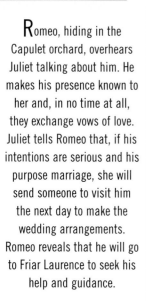

Romeo, hiding in the Capulet orchard, overhears Juliet talking about him. He makes his presence known to her and, in no time at all, they exchange vows of love. Juliet tells Romeo that, if his intentions are serious and his purpose marriage, she will send someone to visit him the next day to make the wedding arrangements. Romeo reveals that he will go to Friar Laurence to seek his help and guidance.

1. *wound* – of love, that is

8. *vestal livery* – virginal clothing

13. *discourses* – speaks

RELATED READING

Who Cannot Recall – poem by Philarete Chasles (page 140)

Act Two
Scene 2

Capulet's orchard.

Enter Romeo.

ROMEO: He jests at scars that never felt a wound.

[Enter Juliet above.]

But soft! What light through yonder window breaks?
It is the east, and Juliet is the sun!
Arise fair sun and kill the envious moon,
Who is already sick and pale with grief
That thou her maid art far more fair than she.
Be not her maid since she is envious.
Her vestal livery is but sick and green
And none but fools do wear it. Cast it off.
It is my lady, O, it is my love!   10
O that she knew she were!
She speaks, yet she says nothing. What of that?
Her eye discourses, I will answer it.
I am too bold. 'Tis not to me she speaks.
Two of the fairest stars in all the heaven,
Having some business, do entreat her eyes
To twinkle in their spheres till they return.
What if her eyes were there, they in her head?
The brightness of her cheek would shame those stars
As daylight doth a lamp. Her eyes in heaven   20
Would through the airy region stream so bright
That birds would sing and think it were not night.
See how she leans her cheek upon her hand.
O that I were a glove upon that hand,
That I might touch that cheek!

JULIET: Ay me!

ROMEO: She speaks.

O, speak again, bright angel, for thou art

As glorious to this night, being over my head,

As is a winged messenger of heaven   30

Unto the white-upturned wondering eyes

Of mortals that fall back to gaze on him

When he bestrides the lazy-puffing clouds

And sails upon the bosom of the air.

JULIET: O Romeo, Romeo, wherefore art thou Romeo?

Deny thy father and refuse thy name.

Or, if thou wilt not, be but sworn my love

And I'll no longer be a Capulet.

ROMEO: Shall I hear more, or shall I speak at this?

JULIET: 'Tis but thy name that is my enemy.   40

Thou art thyself, though not a Montague.

What's Montague? It is nor hand, nor foot,

Nor arm, nor face, nor any other part

Belonging to a man. O, be some other name.

What's in a name? That which we call a rose

By any other name would smell as sweet.

So Romeo would, were he not Romeo called,

Retain that dear perfection which he owes

Without that title. Romeo, doff thy name,

And for that name, which is no part of thee,   50

Take all myself.

ROMEO: I take thee at thy word.

Call me but love, and I'll be new baptized.

Henceforth I never will be Romeo.

JULIET: What man art thou that, thus bescreened in night,

So stumblest on my counsel?

ROMEO: By a name

I know not how to tell thee who I am.

My name, dear saint, is hateful to myself,

Because it is an enemy to thee.   60

Had I it written, I would tear the word.

JULIET: My ears have yet not drunk a hundred words

Of thy tongue's uttering, yet I know the sound.

Art thou not Romeo, and a Montague?

ROMEO: Neither, fair maid, if either thee dislike.

JULIET: How cam'st thou hither, tell me, and wherefore?

The orchard walls are high and hard to climb,

And the place death, considering who thou art,

If any of my kinsmen find thee here.

"To know Juliet as Shakespeare has created her is to love her. For Juliet is love. In her is found all the rare beauty of a first great love, with its purity, its breathless ardor, its eternal truth, its constant devotion, its strength, its weakness, and its courage."
– Norma Shearer, U.S. movie actor

33. *bestrides* – rides as if on a horse

33. *lazy-puffing* – slow moving

35. *wherefore* – why. Juliet is not asking about his location, but rather why his name is Montague.

49. *doff* – cast aside

55. *bescreened* – hidden

56. *counsel* – spoken private thoughts

45

70. *overperch* – fly over

73. *stop* – obstacle

74. *they* – Notice that Juliet, who is in love with Romeo, refers to her kinsmen as *they* already. She is distancing herself from her family because they feel Romeo is their enemy.

82. *prorogued* – postponed

88. *adventure* – take on a perilous journey

92. *Fain ... form* – I would willingly take pains to follow the proper formalities (between lovers)
93. *compliment* – polite formality
96. *perjuries* – lying under oath

97. *Jove* – Jupiter, not only the king of the Roman gods but also the god of oaths and promises. He was reputed to have laughed when lovers broke their vows to each other.

105. *strange* – aloof, distant
107. *ware* – aware
109. *impute* – attribute
110. *discovered* – revealed

ROMEO: With love's light wings did I overperch these walls,   70
    For stony limits cannot hold love out,
    And what love can do, that dares love attempt.
    Therefore thy kinsmen are no stop to me.
JULIET: If they do see thee, they will murder thee.
ROMEO: Alack, there lies more peril in thine eye
    Than twenty of their swords. Look thou but sweet,
    And I am proof against their enmity.
JULIET: I would not for the world they saw thee here.
ROMEO: I have night's cloak to hide me from their eyes,
    And but thou love me, let them find me here.   80
    My life were better ended by their hate
    Than death prorogued, wanting of thy love.
JULIET: By whose direction foundest thou out this place?
ROMEO: By love, that first did prompt me to enquire.
    He lent me counsel, and I lent him eyes.
    I am no pilot, yet, wert thou as far
    As that vast shore washed with the farthest sea,
    I should adventure for such merchandise.
JULIET: Thou knowest the mask of night is on my face,
    Else would a maiden blush bepaint my cheek   90
    For that which thou hast heard me speak tonight.
    Fain would I dwell on form – fain, fain deny
    What I have spoke. But farewell compliment.
    Dost thou love me? I know thou wilt say "Ay,"
    And I will take thy word. Yet, if thou swearest,
    Thou mayst prove false. At lovers' perjuries,
    They say Jove laughs. O gentle Romeo,
    If thou dost love, pronounce it faithfully.
    Or if thou thinkest I am too quickly won,
    I'll frown and be perverse and say thee nay,   100
    So thou wilt woo. But else, not for the world.
    In truth, fair Montague, I am too fond,
    And therefore thou mayst think my haviour light,
    But trust me, gentleman, I'll prove more true
    Than those that have more cunning to be strange.
    I should have been more strange, I must confess,
    But that thou overheardest, ere I was ware,
    My true-love passion. Therefore pardon me,
    And not impute this yielding to light love,
    Which the dark night hath so discovered.   110
ROMEO: Lady, by yonder blessed moon I vow,
    That tips with silver all these fruit-tree tops —

JULIET: O, swear not by the moon, the inconstant moon,
    That monthly changes in her circled orb,
    Lest that thy love prove likewise variable.
ROMEO: What shall I swear by?
JULIET: Do not swear at all.
    Or if thou wilt, swear by thy gracious self,
    Which is the god of my idolatry,
    And I'll believe thee.   120
ROMEO: If my heart's dear love —
JULIET: Well, do not swear. Although I joy in thee,
    I have no joy of this contract tonight.
    It is too rash, too unadvised, too sudden,
    Too like the lightning, which doth cease to be
    Ere one can say "It lightens." Sweet, good night.
    This bud of love, by summer's ripening breath,
    May prove a beauteous flower when next we meet.
    Good night, good night. As sweet repose and rest
    Come to thy heart as that within my breast.   130
ROMEO: O, wilt thou leave me so unsatisfied?
JULIET: What satisfaction canst thou have tonight?
ROMEO: The exchange of thy love's faithful vow for mine.
JULIET: I gave thee mine before thou didst request it,
    And yet I would it were to give again.
ROMEO: Wouldst thou withdraw it? For what purpose, love?
JULIET: But to be frank and give it thee again.
    And yet I wish but for the thing I have.
    My bounty is as boundless as the sea,
    My love as deep. The more I give to thee,   140
    The more I have, for both are infinite.
    I hear some noise within. Dear love, adieu.

[Nurse calls within.]

Anon, good nurse! Sweet Montague, be true.
Stay but a little, I will come again.

[Exit Juliet.]

ROMEO: O blessed, blessed night! I am afeard,
    Being in night, all this is but a dream,
    Too flattering-sweet to be substantial.

[Enter Juliet above.]

119. *idolatry* – worship
122. *joy* – rejoice
123. *contract* – exchange of vows

124. *It is too rash – Morality plays,* popular in the early sixteenth century, taught moral lessons through the use of simple plots and characters. Many commentators have remarked that Shakespeare's tragedies (besides being rich, complex works) are also sophisticated morality plays. Juliet here introduces what will prove to be the most important of lessons to be learned in this play – the dangers of haste.

137. *frank* – open, generous
139. *bounty* – generous offering of love

"Possibly one of the most important aspects of Juliet is her youth…. When she meets Romeo at her parents' party and responds to him so fully, so utterly, she decides, like a child might, that this is it, that there will be no other lover for her, that she is wedded now for life, with a kind of single-mindedness that only innocents are capable of….
    You might say that the tragedy of Juliet and her Romeo begins when Romeo, hiding in the orchard, hears what Juliet would never have told him to his face in the light of day, that she has devoted herself to him utterly."
– Germaine Greer (b. 1939), Australian author and educator

Act Two • Scene 2

RELATED READING

What the Moon Saw –
poem by Hans Christian
Andersen (page 141)

165 – 166. It is appropriate
for Romeo, who is perhaps not
much older than fifteen, to use
this school analogy to describe
lovers' meetings and partings.

168. *tassel-gentle* – noble
peregrine falcon
169. "Being under the
control of my father prevents
me from speaking loudly."

170 – 173. Juliet claims
that if she were free of her
father's control, she would
spend her time repeating
Romeo's name over and over
again. *Echo* was a mountain
nymph who lived in a cave.
She fell in love with Narcissus,
but he was not interested in
her. She pined away and
eventually became nothing
more than a voice, an echo.

178. *nyas* – young hawk

JULIET: Three words, dear Romeo, and good night indeed.
If that thy bent of love be honourable,
Thy purpose marriage, send me word tomorrow,   150
By one that I'll procure to come to thee,
Where and what time thou wilt perform the rite,
And all my fortunes at thy foot I'll lay
And follow thee my lord throughout the world.
NURSE: *[Within.]* Madam!
JULIET: I come, anon — But if thou meanest not well,
I do beseech thee —
NURSE: *[Within.]* Madam!
JULIET: By and by I come. —
To cease thy strife and leave me to my grief.   160
Tomorrow will I send.
ROMEO: So thrive my soul —
JULIET: A thousand times good night!

[Exit Juliet.]

ROMEO: A thousand times the worse, to want thy light.
Love goes toward love as schoolboys from their books,
But love from love, towards school with heavy looks.

Enter Juliet [above] again.

JULIET: Hist! Romeo, hist! O for a falconer's voice
To lure this tassel-gentle back again.
Bondage is hoarse and may not speak aloud,
Else would I tear the cave where Echo lies,   170
And make her airy tongue more hoarse than mine
With repetition of my Romeo's name.
Romeo!
ROMEO: It is my soul that calls upon my name.
How silver-sweet sound lovers' tongues by night,
Like softest music to attending ears.
JULIET: Romeo.
ROMEO: My nyas?
JULIET: At what o'clock tomorrow
Shall I send to thee?   180
ROMEO: By the hour of nine.
JULIET: I will not fail. 'Tis twenty years till then.
I have forgot why I did call thee back.
ROMEO: Let me stand here till thou remember it.
JULIET: I shall forget, to have thee still stand there,
Remembering how I love thy company.

ROMEO: And I'll still stay, to have thee still forget,
 Forgetting any other home but this.
JULIET: 'Tis almost morning. I would have thee gone,
 And yet no farther than a wanton's bird,   190
 That lets it hop a little from his hand,
 Like a poor prisoner in his twisted gyves,
 And with a silk thread plucks it back again,
 So loving-jealous of his liberty.
ROMEO: I would I were thy bird.
JULIET: Sweet, so would I.
 Yet I should kill thee with much cherishing.
 Good night, good night! Parting is such sweet sorrow,
 That I shall say good night till it be morrow.
ROMEO: Sleep dwell upon thine eyes, peace in thy breast.   200
 Would I were sleep and peace, so sweet to rest.

[Exit Juliet.]

Hence will I to my ghostly father's cell,
His help to crave and my dear hap to tell.

Exit.

190. *wanton's bird* – a bird (child) that has been spoiled by an overly protective person
192. *gyves* – fetters; shackles

gyves

202. *ghostly father's cell* – spiritual father's private quarters
203. *dear hap* – good fortune

It is very early Monday morning. As Friar Laurence picks his flowers and herbs, he reflects upon the dual nature of plants and people, in that both have the potential for good and evil. Romeo informs the Friar of his love for Juliet and asks him to marry them later that day. The Friar is at first reluctant, but soon agrees to perform the ceremony in the hope that this marriage will end the feud between the two families.

3. *flecked* – dabbled with red patches (like a drunkard's face)
4. "Out of the way of Titan, the Greek sun-god's chariot."
7. *osier cage* – willow basket
8. *baleful* – poisonous, evil
9 – 10. "The earth is both mother and tomb of all life. What dies returns to earth, and in turn becomes new life."
11. *divers* – different
13. *virtues* – healing properties of plants
15. *mickle* – great
15. *grace* – divine healing power
17. *naught* – nothing is
19 – 20. "Nor is there anything so good that it cannot be perverted from its natural fair qualities and be used for ill."
22. "And evil can sometimes be seen as worthy when it results in a good act."

Act Two
Scene 3

Friar Laurence's cell.

Enter Friar [Laurence] alone, with a basket.

FRIAR: The grey-eyed morn smiles on the frowning night,
    Check'ring the eastern clouds with streaks of light;
    And flecked darkness like a drunkard reels
    From forth day's path and Titan's fiery wheels.
    Now, ere the sun advance his burning eye
    The day to cheer and night's dank dew to dry,
    I must up-fill this osier cage of ours
    With baleful weeds and precious-juiced flowers.
    The earth that's nature's mother is her tomb.
    What is her burying grave, that is her womb;   10
    And from her womb children of divers kind
    We sucking on her natural bosom find.
    Many for many virtues excellent,
    None but for some, and yet all different.
    O, mickle is the powerful grace that lies
    In plants, herbs, stones, and their true qualities.
    For naught so vile that on the earth doth live
    But to the earth some special good doth give;
    Nor aught so good but, strained from that fair use,
    Revolts from true birth, stumbling on abuse.   20
    Virtue itself turns vice, being misapplied,
    And vice sometime's by action dignified.

Enter Romeo [unseen by Friar Laurence].

Within the infant rind of this small flower
Poison hath residence, and medicine power;
For this, being smelt, with that part cheers each part;

Being tasted, stays all senses with the heart.
Two such opposed kings encamp them still
In man as well as herbs — grace and rude will;
And where the worser is predominant,
Full soon the canker death eats up that plant.　　　30
ROMEO:　Good morrow, father.
FRIAR:　Benedicite!
　　What early tongue so sweet saluteth me?
　　Young son, it argues a distempered head
　　So soon to bid good morrow to thy bed.
　　Care keeps his watch in every old man's eye,
　　And where care lodges sleep will never lie,
　　But where unbruised youth with unstuffed brain
　　Doth couch his limbs, there golden sleep doth reign.
　　Therefore thy earliness doth me assure　　　40
　　Thou art uproused with some distemperature.
　　Or if not so, then here I hit it right —
　　Our Romeo hath not been in bed tonight.
ROMEO:　That last is true — the sweeter rest was mine.
FRIAR:　God pardon sin! Wast thou with Rosaline?
ROMEO:　With Rosaline! My ghostly father, no.
　　I have forgot that name, and that name's woe.
FRIAR:　That's my good son! But where hast thou been then?
ROMEO:　I'll tell thee ere thou ask it me again.
　　I have been feasting with mine enemy,　　　50
　　Where on a sudden one hath wounded me
　　That's by me wounded. Both our remedies
　　Within thy help and holy physic lies.
　　I bear no hatred, blessed man, for, lo,
　　My intercession likewise steads my foe.
FRIAR:　Be plain, good son, and homely in thy drift.
　　Riddling confession finds but riddling shrift.
ROMEO:　Then plainly know my heart's dear love is set
　　On the fair daughter of rich Capulet.
　　As mine on hers, so hers is set on mine,　　　60
　　And all combined, save what thou must combine
　　By holy marriage. When, and where, and how
　　We met, we wooed, and made exchange of vow,
　　I'll tell thee as we pass. But this I pray,
　　That thou consent to marry us today.
FRIAR:　Holy Saint Francis! What a change is here!
　　Is Rosaline, that thou didst love so dear,
　　So soon forsaken? Young men's love then lies
　　Not truly in their hearts, but in their eyes.
　　Jesu Maria! What a deal of brine　　　70

26. *stays* – stops
27. *kings* – powers
28. *rude will* – desires of the flesh
30. *canker* – cancer; caterpillar
32. *Benedicite* – Latin for "Bless you"
34. *distempered head* – disturbed mind
35. *good morrow* – goodbye
36. *Care ... watch* – worry keeps an old man ever alert or awake
38. *unbruised youth* – youth unhurt by life's experiences
38. *unstuffed* – absence of troubles
41. *distemperature* – unease, discomfort of mind
46. *ghostly* – spiritual

53. *physic* – healing power (sacrament of marriage)
55. *intercession* – prayer
55. *steads* – benefits
56. *homely* – plain
57. *Riddling* – ambiguous, unclear
57. *shrift* – absolution; spiritual advice

70. *brine* – salty tears

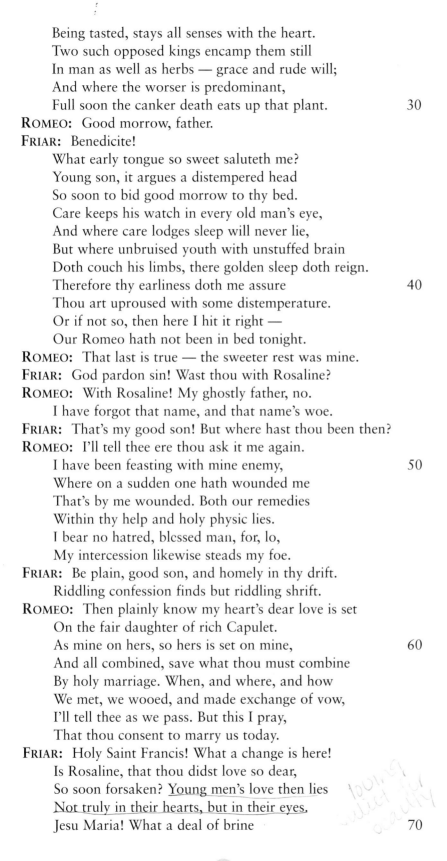

71. *sallow* – pale

73. "To preserve a love that was not love at all."

80. *sentence* – maxim; wise saying
81. *may fall* – can be excused for weakness
82. *chid'st* – scolded
86. "To bury one love, only to find another."
88. *allow* – return
91. *rote* – memory
91. "You love like one who recites from a book without the ability to understand what you memorize."
92. *waverer* – changeable one
95. *rancour* – hate
96. *stand* – insist

97. This proverb reiterates the moral lesson that the Elizabethans would have derived from this story.

Did you notice that the entire scene is written in rhyming couplets? This is evidence that this play is an early work in Shakespeare's career. As his mastery developed, his use of rhyme decreased.

Hath washed thy sallow cheeks for Rosaline.
How much salt water thrown away in waste,
To season love, that of it doth not taste.
The sun not yet thy sighs from heaven clears,
Thy old groans ring yet in mine ancient ears.
Lo, here upon thy cheek the stain doth sit
Of an old tear that is not washed off yet.
If ever thou wast thyself, and these woes thine,
Thou and these woes were all for Rosaline.
And art thou changed? Pronounce this sentence then: 80
Women may fall when there's no strength in men.
ROMEO: Thou chid'st me oft for loving Rosaline.
FRIAR: For doting, not for loving, pupil mine.
ROMEO: And bad'st me bury love.
FRIAR: Not in a grave
    To lay one in, another out to have.
ROMEO: I pray thee chide me not. Her I love now
    Doth grace for grace and love for love allow.
    The other did not so.
FRIAR: O, she knew well   90
    Thy love did read by rote, that could not spell.
    But come, young waverer, come go with me.
    In one respect I'll thy assistant be,
    For this alliance may so happy prove
    To turn your households' rancour to pure love.
ROMEO: O, let us hence! I stand on sudden haste.
FRIAR: Wisely, and slow. They stumble that run fast.

Exeunt.

slow down, the relationship may fall apart

Act Two
Scene 4

A street.

Enter Benvolio and Mercutio.

MERCUTIO: Where the devil should this Romeo be? Came he not home tonight?

BENVOLIO: Not to his father's. I spoke with his man.

MERCUTIO: Why, that same pale hard-hearted wench, that Rosaline, torments him so that he will sure run mad.

BENVOLIO: Tybalt, the kinsman to old Capulet, hath sent a letter to his father's house.

MERCUTIO: A challenge, on my life.

BENVOLIO: Romeo will answer it.

MERCUTIO: Any man that can write may answer a letter.   10

BENVOLIO: Nay, he will answer the letter's master, how he dares, being dared.

MERCUTIO: Alas, poor Romeo, he is already dead! Stabbed with a white wench's black eye, shot through the ear with a love song, the very pin of his heart cleft with the blind bow-boy's butt-shaft. And is he a man to encounter Tybalt?

BENVOLIO: Why, what is Tybalt?

MERCUTIO: More than Prince of Cats. O, he's the courageous captain of compliments. He fights as you sing pricksong,   20 keeps time, distance, and proportion. He rests his minim rests, one, two, and the third in your bosom. The very butcher of a silk button, a duellist, a duellist! A gentleman of the very first house, of the first and second cause. Ah, the immortal *passado*, the *punto reverso*, the *hay*!

BENVOLIO: The what?

Mercutio and Benvolio discuss Tybalt, who has sent a challenge to Romeo's house. Romeo arrives and engages in a battle of wits with Mercutio. Juliet's Nurse and Romeo together establish that Juliet will go to Friar Laurence's cell later that afternoon, where she and Romeo will be married.

15. *pin* – wooden peg found in the centre of an archery target

16. *blind … butt-shaft* – Cupid's heavy but accurate arrow

19. *Prince of Cats* – Tybert is the name of the prince of cats in the medieval fable, *Reynard the Fox.*

20. *pricksong* – printed music

21 – 22. *proportion … minim rests* – rhythm … briefest note in music

23. *butcher … button* – Mercutio is sarcastically praising Tybalt's skill and accuracy as a swordsman.

24. *first house* – highest rank

24 – 25. *first and second cause* – Duellists ranked the various causes for which one would enter a duel.

25. *passado* – forward thrust

25. *punto reverso* – back-handed thrust

26. *hay* – When a thrust hits the opponent, one shouts "hai," which is Italian for "thou hast it."

28 – 29. "A plague upon such ridiculous, lisping, snobbish fools."

32. *strange flies* – foreign parasites

35. *bones* – a pun on the French *bon,* which would have been another over-used phrase like *pardon-me* to which Mercutio objects

37. *roe* – fish eggs; pun on Romeo's name

38 – 40. *Now ... her* – Petrarch (1304 – 1374) was the inventor of the sonnet form. His poems expressed the idea of courtly love.

40 – 43. Each of the women who Mercutio mentions was a famous lover whose story ended tragically.

41 – 42. *dowdy ... hildings and harlots* – plain ... worth-less creatures and prostitutes

44. *counterfeit* – play on the word "slip," which was an Elizabethan expression for counterfeit coin

48. *conceive* – comprehend

52. *bow in the hams* – bend at the knees

59. *pump* – shoe

63. *singleness* – silliness is meant

65. *Switch ... match* – Romeo exhorts Mercutio to spur on his wits, or he will declare himself victor in this war of wits.

69. *goose* – i.e., "fool"

MERCUTIO: The pox of such antic, lisping, affecting fantasticoes, these new tuners of accent! "By Jesu, a very good blade! A very tall man! A very good whore!" Why, is not this a lamentable thing, grandsire, that we should be thus afflicted with these strange flies, these fashion-mongers, these pardon-me's, who stand so much on the new form that they cannot sit at ease on the old bench? O, their bones, their bones!   30

Enter Romeo.

BENVOLIO: Here comes Romeo! Here comes Romeo!

MERCUTIO: Without his roe, like a dried herring. O flesh, flesh, how art thou fishified! Now is he for the numbers that Petrarch flowed in. Laura, to his lady, was a kitchen wench — marry, she had a better love to berhyme her — Dido a dowdy, Cleopatra a gypsy, Helen and Hero hildings and harlots, Thisbe a grey eye or so, but not to the purpose. Signior Romeo, *bonjour.* There's a French salutation to your French slop. You gave us the counterfeit fairly last night.   40

ROMEO: Good morrow to you both. What counterfeit did I give you?

MERCUTIO: The slip, sir, the slip. Can you not conceive?

ROMEO: Pardon, good Mercutio. My business was great, and in such a case as mine a man may strain courtesy.   50

MERCUTIO: That's as much as to say, such a case as yours constrains a man to bow in the hams.

ROMEO: Meaning, to curtsy.

MERCUTIO: Thou hast most kindly hit it.

ROMEO: A most courteous exposition.

MERCUTIO: Nay, I am the very pink of courtesy.

ROMEO: Pink for flower.

MERCUTIO: Right.

ROMEO: Why, then is my pump well-flowered.

MERCUTIO: Sure wit, follow me this jest now, till thou hast worn out thy pump, that when the single sole of it is worn, the jest may remain, after the wearing, solely singular.   60

ROMEO: O single-soled jest, solely singular for the singleness!

MERCUTIO: Come between us, good Benvolio! My wits faint.

ROMEO: Switch and spurs, switch and spurs, or I'll cry a match.

MERCUTIO: Nay, if our wits run the wild-goose chase, I am done; for thou hast more of the wild goose in one of thy wits than, I am sure, I have in my whole five. Was I with you there for the goose?

ROMEO: Thou wast never with me for anything when thou   70
  wast not there for the goose.

MERCUTIO: I will bite thee by the ear for that jest.

ROMEO: Nay, good goose, bite not!

MERCUTIO: Thy wit is a very bitter sweeting. It is a most sharp
  sauce.

ROMEO: And is it not then well served in to a sweet goose?

MERCUTIO: O, here's a wit of cheveril, that stretches from an
  inch narrow to an ell broad!

ROMEO: I stretch it out for that word "broad," which, added   80
  to the goose, proves thee far and wide a broad goose.

MERCUTIO: Why, is not this better now than groaning for
  love? Now art thou sociable, now art thou Romeo. Now
  art thou what thou art, by art as well as by nature. For
  this drivelling love is like a great natural that runs lolling
  up and down to hide his bauble in a hole.

BENVOLIO: Stop there, stop there!

MERCUTIO: Thou desirest me to stop in my tale against the
  hair.

BENVOLIO: Thou wouldst else have made thy tale large.

MERCUTIO: O, thou art deceived! I would have made it short,   90
  for I was come to the whole depth of my tale and meant
  indeed to occupy the argument no longer.

ROMEO: Here's goodly gear!

Enter Nurse and her man [Peter].

MERCUTIO: A sail, a sail!

BENVOLIO: Two, two! A shirt and a smock.

NURSE: Peter!

PETER: Anon.

NURSE: My fan, Peter.

MERCUTIO: Good Peter, to hide her face, for her fan's the
  fairer face.   100

NURSE: God ye good morrow, gentlemen.

MERCUTIO: God ye good-den, fair gentlewoman.

NURSE: Is it good-den?

MERCUTIO: 'Tis no less, I tell ye, for the bawdy hand of the
  dial is now upon the prick of noon.

NURSE: Out upon you! What a man are you!

ROMEO: One, gentlewoman, that God hath made for himself
  to mar.

NURSE: By my troth, it is well said. "For himself to mar,"
  quoth he? Gentlemen, can any of you tell me where I may   110
  find the young Romeo?

77. *cheveril* – soft leather that is easily stretched
78. *ell* – 110 cm or 45 inches
77 – 78. Mercutio implies that Romeo can make his little wit stretch a long way.
84. *natural* – idiot; fool
87 – 88. "You want me to stop just when I was getting to the point?"

93. *goodly gear* – fine entertainment
95. *shirt ... smock* – a man and a woman
102. *good-den* – good evening
105. *prick of noon* – point on the dial of a clock

"If there is one thing which Shakespeare has been stressing about Tybalt (and hence one thing which would have caught the eye of his audience), it is the lava-like quality of his temperament. He is hate personified. He is grim. He is deadly. In short, he is anything but what Mercutio says he is, a perfumed dandy who minces his way across the stage."
– James H. Seward, scholar

114. *fault ... worse* – for want of a better

118. *confidence* – What the Nurse really means is "conference." In unknowingly substituting an inappropriate word that is similar to the correct word, the Nurse is guilty of *malapropism.* Shakespeare has many of his characters use malapropisms for comical effect. Benvolio, realizing that the Nurse has used the wrong word, offers his own malapropism in the next line when he says *endite* instead of *invite. Endite* means *write.*

120. *bawd* – procuress; one who operates a house of prostitution

122 – 123. *lenten ... spent* – During Lent meat was not supposed to be eaten. However, some would sneak some rabbit in a pie and eat at it sparingly. In no time it would go mouldy and stale.

123. *hoar* – grey, mouldy

129. *spent* – used up, eaten

134. *lady, lady, lady* – line from a popular ballad, sung by Mercutio sarcastically

136. *ropery* – indecent jesting

140. *And* – if

143 – 144. *flirt-gills ... skain-mates* – loose women ... cutthroats

145. *suffer* – allow

ROMEO: I can tell you, but young Romeo will be older when you have found him than he was when you sought him. I am the youngest of that name, for fault of a worse.

NURSE: You say well.

MERCUTIO: Yea, is the worst well? Very well took, in faith. Wisely, wisely.

NURSE: If you be he sir, I desire some confidence with you.

BENVOLIO: She will endite him to some supper.

MERCUTIO: A bawd, a bawd, a bawd! So ho! 120

ROMEO: What hast thou found?

MERCUTIO: No hare, sir, unless a hare, sir, in a lenten pie, that is something stale and hoar ere it be spent —

He walks by them and sings.

An old hare hoar,
And an old hare hoar,
Is very good meat in Lent.
But a hare that is hoar
Is too much for a score
When it hoars ere it be spent.

Romeo, will you come to your father's? We'll to dinner 130 thither.

ROMEO: I will follow you.

MERCUTIO: Farewell, ancient lady. Farewell,
[*Sings.*] lady, lady, lady.

Exeunt Mercutio, Benvolio.

NURSE: I pray you, sir, what saucy merchant was this that was so full of his ropery?

ROMEO: A gentleman, Nurse, that loves to hear himself talk and will speak more in a minute than he will stand to in a month.

NURSE: And he speak anything against me, I'll take him 140 down, and he were lustier than he is, and twenty such Jacks. And if I cannot, I'll find those that shall. Scurvy knave! I am none of his flirt-gills. I am none of his skains-mates. [*To Peter.*] And thou must stand by too, and suffer every knave to use me at his pleasure!

PETER: I saw no man use you at his pleasure. If I had, my weapon should quickly have been out, I warrant you. I dare draw as soon as another man, if I see occasion in a good quarrel, and the law on my side.

NURSE: Now, afore God, I am so vexed that every part about me quivers. Scurvy knave! Pray you, sir, a word, and, as I told you, my young lady bid me enquire you out. What she bid me say, I will keep to myself, but first let me tell ye, if ye should lead her into a fool's paradise, as they say, it were a very gross kind of behaviour, as they say. For the gentlewoman is young, and therefore, if you should deal double with her, truly it were an ill thing to be offered to any gentlewoman, and very weak dealing. 150

ROMEO: Nurse, commend me to thy lady and mistress. I protest unto thee — 160

NURSE: Good heart, and in faith I will tell her as much. Lord, Lord, she will be a joyful woman.

ROMEO: What wilt thou tell her, Nurse? Thou dost not mark me.

NURSE: I will tell her, sir, that you do protest, which, as I take it, is a gentlemanlike offer.

ROMEO: Bid her devise
Some means to come to shrift this afternoon,
And there she shall at Friar Laurence' cell
Be shrived and married. Here is for thy pains. 170

NURSE: No, truly, sir. Not a penny.

ROMEO: Go to, I say you shall.

NURSE: This afternoon, sir? Well, she shall be there.

ROMEO: And stay, good Nurse, behind the abbey wall.
Within this hour my man shall be with thee
And bring thee cords made like a tackled stair,
Which to the high topgallant of my joy
Must be my convoy in the secret night.
Farewell, be trusty, and I'll quit thy pains.
Farewell. Commend me to thy mistress. 180

NURSE: Now God in heaven bless thee! Hark you, sir.

ROMEO: What sayest thou, my dear nurse?

NURSE: Is your man secret? Did you never hear say,
Two may keep counsel, putting one away?

ROMEO: I warrant thee my man's as true as steel.

NURSE: Well, sir, my mistress is the sweetest lady. Lord, Lord! When 'twas a little prating thing — O, there is a nobleman in town, one Paris, that would fain lay knife aboard; but she, good soul, had as lief see a toad, a very toad, as see him. I anger her sometimes, and tell her that Paris is the properer man, but I'll warrant you, when I say so, she looks as pale as any clout in the versal world. Doth not rosemary and Romeo begin both with a letter? 190

154. *fool's paradise* – state of being deceived and taken advantage of

158. *weak* – contemptible. The Nurse probably should have said "wicked."

159. *commend me* – send my greetings

163. *mark* – listen to

168. *shrift* – confession; church

170. *shrived* – absolved of sins through confession. This would be necessary before receiving the sacrament of marriage.

176. *tackled stair* – rope ladder

177. *topgallant* – summit

178. *convoy* – means of access to Juliet's chamber

179. *quit thy pains* – reward you for your efforts

183. *secret* – able to be trusted

187. *prating* – chattering

188 – 189. *would … aboard* – a reference to the custom of guests bringing their own knives to mark their places at the dinner table and ensuring that they get a helping of the meat. In other words, Paris would like very much to secure his right to marrying Juliet.

189. *had as lief* – would be just as happy to

192. *clout* – rag

192. *versal* – whole; universal

187 – 192. The Nurse talks
as if she has known about
Juliet's relationship with
Romeo for quite some time.
However, she could only have
known of it for several hours.
In Shakespeare's source,
Romeus and Juliet, the lovers
meet at Christmas and marry
close to Easter. Shakespeare
compresses time in his play to
create a more dramatic effect.

197. *sententious* – another
malapropism. The Nurse
most likely means to say
"sentence," which means a
wise saying.

197. *rosemary* – flower
symbolic of remembrance;
it was used at both weddings
and funerals

rosemary

202. *apace* – quickly

ROMEO: Ay, nurse. What of that? Both with an R.

NURSE: Ah, mocker! That's the dog's name. R is for the --
No. I know it begins with some other letter — and she
hath the prettiest sententious of it, of you and rosemary,
that it would do you good to hear it.

ROMEO: Commend me to thy lady.

[Exit Romeo.]

NURSE: Ay, a thousand times. Peter!   200

PETER: Anon.

NURSE: Before and apace.

Exeunt.

Act Two
Scene 5

Capulet's orchard.

It is Monday noon. An impatient Juliet anxiously awaits the Nurse's return to learn what Romeo's intentions are. The Nurse arrives and, after much delay, informs Juliet that Romeo has made arrangements for them to be married later that afternoon at Friar Laurence's cell.

Enter Juliet.

JULIET: The clock struck nine when I did send the nurse,
In half an hour she promised to return.
Perchance she cannot meet him. That's not so.
O, she is lame. Love's heralds should be thoughts
Which ten times faster glide than the sun's beams
Driving back shadows over louring hills.
Therefore do nimble-pinioned doves draw Love,
And therefore hath the wind-swift Cupid wings.
Now is the sun upon the highmost hill
Of this day's journey, and from nine till twelve   10
Is three long hours, yet she is not come.
Had she affections and warm youthful blood,
She would be as swift in motion as a ball.
My words would bandy her to my sweet love,
And his to me,
But old folks, many feign as they were dead —
Unwieldy, slow, heavy and pale as lead.

Enter Nurse [and Peter].

O God, she comes! O honey Nurse, what news?
Hast thou met with him? Send thy man away.
NURSE: Peter, stay at the gate.   20

[Exit Peter.]

JULIET: Now good sweet Nurse — O Lord why lookest
        thou sad?
Though news be sad, yet tell them merrily,
If good, thou shamest the music of sweet news
By playing it to me with so sour a face.

1. *nine* – In the previous scene, the Nurse meets with Romeo at noon. No information is provided as to what the Nurse did for the missing three hours.

4. *heralds* – messengers; go-betweens
6. *louring* – gloomy; threatening

7. *doves draw Love* – Venus, goddess of love, is often depicted riding in a chariot pulled by doves.

12. *affections* – feelings, sensitivity
14. *bandy* – strike; rebound as in a tennis game between players
16. *feign* – act as if

"Romeo represents the *sentiment*, and Juliet the *passion* of love. The *pathos* is his, the *power* hers."
– Frances Anne Kemble (1809 – 1893), English actor and author

59

26. *jaunce* – perhaps she means "jaunt" or tiring trip

29. *what haste!* – Notice again the reference to one of the more important themes in the play: haste. Ultimately this haste, this impatience, will lead to the tragedy at the end of the play.

RELATED READING

Juliet and her nurse – poem by John Wain (page 148)

36. *stay the circumstance* – wait for the details of the news
38. *simple* – foolish
43. *warrant* – vouch for

"The nurse is one of the characters in which the author delighted; he has, with great subtlety of distinction, drawn her at once loquacious and secret, obsequious and insolent, trusty and dishonest."
– Samuel Johnson (1709 – 1784), British essayist, biographer, and developer of the first true English dictionary

50. *Beshrew your heart* – shame on you

NURSE: I am aweary, give me leave awhile.
    Fie, how my bones ache! What a jaunce have I had!
JULIET: I would thou hadst my bones, and I thy news.
    Nay come, I pray thee speak. Good, good Nurse, speak.
NURSE: Jesu, what haste! Can you not stay awhile?
    Do you not see that I am out of breath?   30
JULIET: How art thou out of breath when thou hast breath
    To say to me that thou art out of breath?
    The excuse that thou dost make in this delay
    Is longer than the tale thou dost excuse.
    Is thy news good or bad? Answer to that.
    Say either, and I'll stay the circumstance.
    Let me be satisfied, is it good or bad?
NURSE: Well, you have made a simple choice. You know not
    how to choose a man. Romeo? No, not he. Though his
    face be better than any man's, yet his leg excels all men's,   40
    and for a hand and a foot, and a body, though they be
    not to be talked on, yet they are past compare. He is not
    the flower of courtesy, but, I'll warrant him as gentle as
    a lamb. Go thy ways, wench, serve God. What, have you
    dined at home?
JULIET: No, no. But all this did I know before.
    What says he of our marriage? What of that?
NURSE: Lord, how my head aches! What a head have I!
    It beats as it would fall in twenty pieces.
    My back on to other side — ah, my back, my back!
    Beshrew your heart for sending me about   50
    To catch my death with jauncing up and down.

JULIET: In faith, I am sorry that thou art not well.
　　Sweet, sweet, sweet Nurse, tell me, what says my love?
NURSE: Your love says, like an honest gentleman
　　And a courteous, and a kind, and a handsome,
　　And, I warrant, a virtuous — Where is your mother?
JULIET: Where is my mother? Why, she is within.
　　Where should she be? How oddly thou repliest.
　　"Your love says, like an honest gentleman,
　　'Where is your mother?'" 　　　　　　　　　　　60
NURSE: O God's lady dear!
　　Are you so hot? Marry come up, I trow.
　　Is this the poultice for my aching bones?
　　Henceforward do your messages yourself.
JULIET: Here's such a coil! Come, what says Romeo?
NURSE: Have you got leave to go to shrift today?
JULIET: I have.
NURSE: Then hie you hence to Friar Laurence' cell.
　　There stays a husband to make you a wife.
　　Now comes the wanton blood up in your cheeks. 　　70
　　They'll be in scarlet straight at any news.
　　Hie you to church. I must another way
　　To fetch a ladder by the which your love
　　Must climb a bird's nest soon when it is dark.
　　I am the drudge, and toil in your delight,
　　But you shall bear the burden soon at night.
　　Go. I'll to dinner. Hie you to the cell.
JULIET: Hie to high fortune! Honest Nurse, farewell.

Exeunt.

62. *hot* – impatient
62. *trow* – believe
63. *poultice* – medicinal balm
65. *coil* – fuss
66. *leave* – permission
68. *hie* – hurry, get

70. *wanton* – uncontrolled

74. *bird's nest* – Juliet's bedchamber
75. *drudge* – lowly worker

Romeo and Juliet meet and are married at Friar Laurence's cell. It is now Monday afternoon.

Act Two
Scene 6

Friar Laurence's cell.

Enter Friar [Laurence] and Romeo.

1 – 2. "Let Heaven so smile upon this holy act that afterwards no sorrow can make us regret what we have done."
4. *countervail* – equal

FRIAR: So smile the heavens upon this holy act
    That after-hours with sorrow chide us not.
ROMEO: Amen, amen, but come what sorrow can,
    It cannot countervail the exchange of joy
    That one short minute gives me in her sight.
    Do thou but close our hands with holy words,
    Then love-devouring death do what he dare —
    It is enough I may but call her mine.
FRIAR: These violent delights have violent ends

10. *powder* – gunpowder

    And in their triumph die, like fire and powder,   10
    Which as they kiss consume. The sweetest honey
    Is loathsome in his own deliciousness

13. *confounds* – spoils

    And in the taste confounds the appetite.
    Therefore love moderately. Long love doth so.
    Too swift arrives as tardy as too slow.

Enter Juliet, somewhat fast and embraces Romeo.

17. *flint* – path
18. *gossamers* – spider webs
19. *idles ... wanton* – dallies in the playful
20. *so ... vanity* – so trivial is the pursuit of worldly pleasures

    Here comes the lady. O, so light a foot
    Will never wear out the everlasting flint.
    A lover may bestride the gossamers
    That idles in the wanton summer air
    And yet not fall; so light is vanity.   20
JULIET: Good even to my ghostly confessor.
FRIAR: Romeo shall thank thee, daughter, for us both.
JULIET: As much to him, else is his thanks too much.
ROMEO: Ah, Juliet, if the measure of thy joy
    Be heaped like mine, and that thy skill be more

To blazon it, then sweeten with thy breath
This neighbour air, and let rich music's tongue
Unfold the imagined happiness that both
Receive in either by this dear encounter.

JULIET: Conceit more rich in matter than in words   30
Brags of his substance, not of ornament.
They are but beggars that can count their worth,
But my true love is grown to such excess
I cannot sum up sum of half my wealth.

FRIAR: Come, come with me and we will make short work,
For, by your leaves, you shall not stay alone
Till Holy Church incorporate two in one.

[Exeunt.]

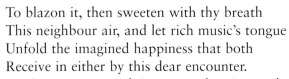

26. *blazon* – announce
27. *neighbour* – surrounding

30. *Conceit* – products of the imagination
31. *ornament* – verbal ostentation; elegant expression
32. "Those who are able to count their wealth are but beggars."
34. *sum up sum* – calculate the total

> "*Romeo and Juliet* is a flawless little jewel of a play. It has the clear, bright colours, the blend of freshness and formality, of an illuminated manuscript. The eagerness and innocence of the young lovers is captured in words that are uncomplicated and memorable, and verse that chimes with a fresh, springy rhythm."
> – John Wain, poet and Shakespeare critic

Act Two Considerations

ACT TWO Prologue

▶ This is the third and final sonnet in the play. Of the three, this sonnet is considered the weakest. Some even doubt that Shakespeare wrote it. Is anything new revealed in this speech? If so, what?

▶ If you were directing a stage version of this play and had to cut lines to shorten the performance, would you keep the prologue? What would be lost or gained by its omission?

ACT TWO Scene 1

▶ How does Mercutio's view of love differ from Romeo's? Create a collage, using illustrations from magazines, that contrasts the two views of love.

ACT TWO Scene 2

▶ Imagine you are a famous daytime talk-show host and you are interviewing the newly engaged Romeo and Juliet. You need, first of all, to create a compelling title for the day's topic. You may use the model: "Teenagers who ..." Then in a series of questions and answers, interview Romeo and Juliet in such a way as to review the information provided in this scene and to encourage them to predict what kinds of consequences their actions might have.

▶ Caroline Spurgeon, in her study of the imagery (page 137) in *Romeo and Juliet,* suggests that many of the images deal with the "glory of sunlight and starlight in a dark world." Another series of images, not dealt with by Spurgeon, are based on ships and navigation. Read this scene carefully and record the many references to these two sets of imagery. What conclusions can you draw based on their usage? In other words, what is Shakespeare trying to say through the use of imagery? How do Romeo and Juliet feel about each other, and how does Romeo feel about his situation?

▶ If you were a playwright and working on a modern-day version of this play, how would you deal with this scene? What changes would you have to make to appeal to today's audiences? For example, what would be the setting? Rewrite the balcony scene for this modern-day version. Do not attempt to translate the lines.

ACT TWO Scene 3

▶ The Friar's first speech presents a long series of contrasts. Divide a page into two columns. Identify as many sets of contrasts as you can. The left column should contain words with positive associations, the right column those with negative associations.

What conclusions can you draw about the Friar based on his first speech?

▶ The Friar criticizes Romeo for being so quick to forget about Rosaline and for falling so quickly in love with Juliet. David Garrick, a famous eighteenth-century Shakespearean actor, also argued that the sudden change in Romeo was "a blemish in his character" and as a result, in his 1750 production of the play, Garrick left out the Rosaline subplot.

Write a short paragraph expressing your opinion of Garrick's decision. What purpose does the Rosaline subplot serve?

▶ The scene ends with a proverb on the dangers of haste. In the ensuing scenes, a number of characters also make proverb-like statements about haste. In your notebook, begin a collection of these proverbs.

▶ If you were a casting director in search of someone to play the Friar, how would you describe the person you are looking for? Write the advertisement. Consider more than just physical characteristics. This ad should take approximately fifty words.

ACT TWO Scene 4

▶ Mercutio, in lines 40 to 42, mentions a number of famous lovers involved in tragic stories. Choose one of these women to research. Create a small poster containing illustrations and a brief summary of her tragic story.

▶ Imagine you are the Nurse and you are quite upset with the way Mercutio treated you on the public street. Write a letter to, or a conversation with, Mercutio's parents in which you describe what happened and how you feel about the incident.

▶ In the latter part of this scene, Romeo and the Nurse finalize plans for the wedding. How much time has passed since Romeo and Juliet first met? In the original source material for this story, Romeo and Juliet meet around Christmas but don't get married till months later at Easter. Comment on the effect created through Shakespeare's compression of time. To what extent do you think it is effective?

▶ This scene is written entirely in prose, as are most scenes involving comic relief. Shakespeare provides his audience with such scenes to relieve the tension that has been building up and to accentuate the intensity of scenes that will follow. Comment on the style of this scene. Did you find it easier to read than poetry? Would it have worked as well if it were written in verse?

ACT TWO Scene 5

▶ The Nurse was gone three hours to complete a task that should have taken half an hour. Why does Shakespeare have Juliet wait so long? What could the Nurse have been doing during that time? Because she does not return immediately with the news, what does this say about the Nurse's character?

▶ Is the Nurse playfully cruel or genuinely tired? Write a short paragraph in which you express an opinion that accounts for the Nurse's reluctance to give Romeo's message to Juliet immediately.

▶ A metaphor is an implied comparison between two unlike things. In lines 9 to 13, Friar Laurence draws two comparisons. Choose one of them and write a short paragraph outlining fully what the two unlike things being compared have in common.

▶ Shakespeare chooses not to show Romeo and Juliet's actual wedding ceremony. Germaine Greer believes that "By doing so, he raises a doubt in the audience's mind that Friar Laurence has done it in the right [or legally binding] way." Write a short paragraph in which you discuss what is gained or lost by not showing the scene.

Act Three
Scene 1

A public place.

It is a hot day, and the hot blood is stirring. In a series of sword fights, Mercutio is killed by Tybalt, and Tybalt in turn is killed by Romeo. The Prince appears and banishes Romeo for his part in the fray. This scene marks the climax of the play, the point at which the fortunes of the tragic heroes begin to decline. It is still Monday afternoon.

Enter Mercutio, Benvolio, and Men.

BENVOLIO: I pray thee, good Mercutio, let's retire.
  The day is hot, the Capels are abroad.
  And if we meet, we shall not escape a brawl,
  For now these hot days is the mad blood stirring.
MERCUTIO: Thou art like one of these fellows that, when he
  enters the confines of a tavern, claps me his sword upon
  the table and says "God send me no need of thee!" and
  by the operation of the second cup draws him on the
  drawer, when indeed there is no need.
BENVOLIO: Am I like such a fellow?   10
MERCUTIO: Come, come, thou art as hot a Jack in thy mood
  as any in Italy; and as soon moved to be moody, and as
  soon moody to be moved.
BENVOLIO: And what to?
MERCUTIO: Nay, and there were two such, we should have
  none shortly, for one would kill the other. Thou, why
  thou wilt quarrel with a man that hath a hair more or a
  hair less in his beard than thou hast. Thou wilt quarrel
  with a man for cracking nuts, having no other reason but
  because thou hast hazel eyes. What eye but such an eye
  would spy out such a quarrel? Thy head is as full of   20
  quarrels as an egg is full of meat, and yet thy head hath
  been beaten as addle as an egg for quarrelling. Thou hast
  quarrelled with a man for coughing in the street, because
  he hath wakened thy dog that hath lain asleep in the sun.
  Didst thou not fall out with a tailor for wearing his new
  doublet before Easter, with another for tying his new
  shoes with an old riband? And yet thou wilt tutor me
  from quarrelling!

1. *retire* – go inside
2. *Capels* – Capulets

4. *mad ... stirring* – It is believed that violent acts are more prone to occur during hot weather. Samuel Johnson wrote that "in Italy almost all assassinations are committed during the heat of summer." Recent historical events may be seen to corroborate this theory.

9. *drawer* – waiter
12. *moved ... moody* – provoked to be angry
21. *meat* – food
22. *addle* – rotten
27. *riband* – ribbon; shoelace

5 – 27. One has to wonder if Mercutio's characterization of Benvolio is accurate. Benvolio means "good will" and his actions seem consistent with his name. If Mercutio's characterization is correct, it would be truly ironic for such a person to be named Benvolio.

30. *fee simple* – rights of possession to
30. *simple* – feeble; foolish

39. *consortest* – associate; are close friends with
40. *Consort* – group of musicians
42. *fiddlestick* – rapier

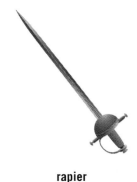

rapier

43. *Zounds* – mild oath, contraction of "by God's wounds"
46. *coldly* – in a cool manner; calmly
51. *wear your livery* – take your insults; act subservient to you

52. *field* – field of battle; site for the duel

57. *appertaining rage* – anger that belongs

63. *devise* – imagine

BENVOLIO: And I were so apt to quarrel as thou art, any man should buy the fee simple of my life for an hour and a quarter.
MERCUTIO: The fee simple? O simple! 30

Enter Tybalt, Petruchio, and others.

BENVOLIO: By my head, here come the Capulets.
MERCUTIO: By my heel, I care not.
TYBALT: Follow me close, for I will speak to them. Gentlemen, good den. A word with one of you.
MERCUTIO: And but one word with one of us? Couple it with something. Make it a word and a blow.
TYBALT: You shall find me apt enough to that, sir, and you will give me occasion.
MERCUTIO: Could you not take some occasion without giving?
TYBALT: Mercutio, thou consortest with Romeo.
MERCUTIO: Consort? What, dost thou make us minstrels? 40 And thou make minstrels of us, look to hear nothing but discords. Here's my fiddlestick, here's that shall make you dance. Zounds, consort!
BENVOLIO: We talk here in the public haunt of men. Either withdraw unto some private place, Or reason coldly of your grievances, Or else depart. Here all eyes gaze on us.
MERCUTIO: Men's eyes were made to look, and let them gaze. I will not budge for no man's pleasure, I.

Enter Romeo.

TYBALT: Well, peace be with you, sir, here comes my man. 50
MERCUTIO: But I'll be hanged, sir, if he wear your livery. Marry, go before to field, he'll be your follower. Your worship in that sense may call him "man."
TYBALT: Romeo, the love I bear thee can afford No better term than this: thou art a villain.
ROMEO: Tybalt, the reason that I have to love thee Doth much excuse the appertaining rage To such a greeting. Villain am I none. Therefore farewell. I see thou knowest me not.
TYBALT: Boy, this shall not excuse the injuries 60 That thou hast done me, therefore turn and draw.
ROMEO: I do protest I never injured thee, But love thee better than thou canst devise

Till thou shalt know the reason of my love.
And so, good Capulet, which name I tender
As dearly as mine own, be satisfied.

MERCUTIO: O calm, dishonourable, vile submission.
Alla stoccata carries it away.

[Draws his sword.]

Tybalt, you ratcatcher, will you walk?

TYBALT: What wouldst thou have with me?   70

MERCUTIO: Good King of Cats, nothing but one of your nine
lives. That I mean to make bold withal, and, as you shall
use me hereafter, dry-beat the rest of the eight. Will you
pluck your sword out of his pilcher by the ears? Make
haste, lest mine be about your ears ere it be out.

TYBALT: I am for you.

[Tybalt draws his sword.]

ROMEO: Gentle Mercutio, put thy rapier up.

MERCUTIO: Come, sir, your *passado*!

[They fight.]

ROMEO: Draw, Benvolio; beat down their weapons.
Gentlemen, for shame, forbear this outrage.   80
Tybalt, Mercutio! The Prince expressly hath
Forbid this bandying in Verona streets.
Hold, Tybalt! Good Mercutio!

Tybalt under Romeo's arm thrusts Mercutio in.

A FOLLOWER: Away Tybalt!

Exit Tybalt [with his Followers].

MERCUTIO: I am hurt.
A plague on both your houses! I am sped.
Is he gone and hath nothing?

BENVOLIO: What, art thou hurt?

MERCUTIO: Ay, ay, a scratch, a scratch. Marry, 'tis enough.
Where is my page? Go, villain, fetch a surgeon.   90

[Exit Page.]

ROMEO: Courage, man. The hurt cannot be much.

68. *Alla stoccata* – Italian
fencing term for "at the
thrust." Mercutio refers to
Tybalt with this expression.
68. *carries it away* – wins the
day

73. *dry-beat* – thrust; beat
without drawing blood
74. *pilcher* – scabbard

pilcher

78. *passado* – thrust
80. *forebear* – put an end to
82. *bandying* – exchanging of
blows

MERCUTIO: No, 'tis not so deep as a well, nor so wide as a church door; but 'tis enough, 'twill serve. Ask for me tomorrow and you shall find me a grave man. I am peppered, I warrant, for this world. A plague on both your houses! Zounds, a dog, a rat, a mouse, a cat, to scratch a man to death! A braggart, a rogue, a villain, that fights by the book of arithmetic! Why the devil came you between us? I was hurt under your arm.

ROMEO: I thought all for the best.

MERCUTIO: Help me into some house, Benvolio,   100
    Or I shall faint. A plague on both your houses!
    They have made worms' meat of me.
    I have it, and soundly too. Your houses!

Exit [Mercutio and Benvolio].

ROMEO: This gentleman, the Prince's near ally,
    My very friend, hath got this mortal hurt
    In my behalf — my reputation stained
    With Tybalt's slander — Tybalt, that an hour
    Hath been my cousin. O sweet Juliet,
    Thy beauty hath made me effeminate
    And in my temper softened valour's steel.   110

Enter Benvolio.

BENVOLIO: O Romeo, Romeo, brave Mercutio is dead.
    That gallant spirit hath aspired the clouds
    Which too untimely here did scorn the earth.

ROMEO: This day's black fate on more days doth depend:
    This but begins the woe others must end.

Enter Tybalt.

BENVOLIO: Here comes the furious Tybalt back again.

ROMEO: Alive, in triumph, and Mercutio slain.
    Away to heaven respective lenity,
    And fire-eyed fury be my conduct now!
    Now, Tybalt, take the "villain" back again   120
    That late thou gavest me, for Mercutio's soul
    Is but a little way above our heads,
    Staying for thine to keep him company.
    Either thou or I, or both, must go with him.

TYBALT: Thou, wretched boy, that didst consort him here,
    Shalt with him hence.

94. *grave* – play on words. Mercutio is dying, but he still finds occasion to pun on the dual meaning of grave.
95. *peppered* – finished
98. *book of arithmetic* – fencing manuals. In other words, Tybalt fights by the formal rules of fencing.
102. *worms' meat* – corpse

110. *temper* – disposition

112. *aspired* – ascended

118. *respective lenity* – gentle considerations (because he is now Tybalt's cousin by marriage)

ROMEO: This shall determine that.

They fight. Tybalt falls.

BENVOLIO: Romeo, away, be gone!
    The citizens are up, and Tybalt slain.
    Stand not amazed. The Prince will doom thee death   130
    If thou art taken. Hence, be gone, away!
ROMEO: O, I am fortune's fool!
BENVOLIO: Why dost thou stay?

Exit Romeo.
Enter Citizens.

CITIZEN: Which way ran he that killed Mercutio?
    Tybalt, that murderer, which way ran he?
BENVOLIO: There lies that Tybalt.
CITIZEN: Up, sir, go with me.
    I charge thee in the Prince's name obey.

Enter Prince, Montague, Capulet, their Wives, and all.

PRINCE: Where are the vile beginners of this fray?
BENVOLIO: O noble Prince. I can discover all   140
    The unlucky manage of this fatal brawl.
    There lies the man, slain by young Romeo,
    That slew thy kinsman, brave Mercutio.
LADY CAPULET: Tybalt, my cousin! O my brother's child!
    O Prince! O husband! O, the blood is spilled
    Of my dear kinsman! Prince, as thou art true,
    For blood of ours shed blood of Montague.
    O cousin, cousin!
PRINCE: Benvolio, who began this bloody fray?
BENVOLIO: Tybalt, here slain, whom Romeo's hand did slay. 150
    Romeo, that spoke him fair, bid him bethink
    How nice the quarrel was, and urged withal
    Your high displeasure. All this uttered
    With gentle breath, calm look, knees humbly bowed,
    Could not take truce with the unruly spleen
    Of Tybalt, deaf to peace, but that he tilts
    With piercing steel at bold Mercutio's breast,
    Who, all as hot, turns deadly point to point
    And, with a martial scorn, with one hand beats
    Cold death aside and with the other sends   160
    It back to Tybalt, whose dexterity

132. *fortune's fool* – victim of fate. We were told by the Chorus that Romeo and Juliet are "star-crossed lovers."

140. *discover* – reveal
141. *manage* – course of events

150. When asked who began the conflict, Benvolio lies, by omission. Was it not Mercutio who challenged Tybalt first? Tybalt was set to challenge Romeo, but the course of events that led to the two deaths was commenced by Mercutio. Why does Benvolio lie? Why does the author have Benvolio unexplainedly disappear forever at the end of this scene? Perhaps Benvolio's last line in this speech has a secondary significance.

152. *nice* – trivial
155. *spleen* – temper

Act Three • Scene 1

162. *retorts* – returns

166. *envious* – hate-filled

187. Notice the switch from "we" to the more personal "I" when the Prince begins to talk of the loss of his relative, Mercutio.

189. *amerce* – punish, usually by charging a fine

196. *Mercy but murders* – Being merciful to murderers encourages others to murder

Retorts it. Romeo, he cries aloud
"Hold, friends! Friends, part!" and swifter than his tongue,
His agile arm beats down their fatal points
And 'twixt them rushes; underneath whose arm
An envious thrust from Tybalt hit the life
Of stout Mercutio; and then Tybalt fled,
But by and by comes back to Romeo,
Who had but newly entertained revenge,
And to it they go like lightning. For, ere I   170
Could draw to part them, was stout Tybalt slain,
And, as he fell, did Romeo turn and fly.
This is the truth, or let Benvolio die.

LADY CAPULET: He is a kinsman to the Montague.
Affection makes him false. He speaks not true.
Some twenty of them fought in this black strife
And all those twenty could but kill one life.
I beg for justice, which thou, Prince, must give.
Romeo slew Tybalt. Romeo must not live.

PRINCE: Romeo slew him, he slew Mercutio.   180
Who now the price of his dear blood doth owe?

MONTAGUE: Not Romeo, Prince, he was Mercutio's friend.
His fault concludes but what the law should end,
The life of Tybalt.

PRINCE: And for that offence
Immediately we do exile him hence.
I have an interest in your hearts' proceeding,
My blood for your rude brawls doth lie a-bleeding.
But I'll amerce you with so strong a fine
That you shall all repent the loss of mine.   190
I will be deaf to pleading and excuses;
Nor tears nor prayers shall purchase out abuses.
Therefore use none. Let Romeo hence in haste,
Else, when he is found, that hour is his last.
Bear hence this body, and attend our will.
Mercy but murders, pardoning those that kill.

Exeunt.

Act Three
Scene 2

Capulet's orchard.

Juliet anxiously awaits the coming of night so that she can see her Romeo. The Nurse arrives with news that Tybalt is dead and Romeo is banished. Juliet, heartbroken over Romeo's exile, is prepared to die. The Nurse informs her that Romeo will visit her chamber that night.

Enter Juliet alone.

JULIET: Gallop apace, you fiery-footed steeds,
Towards Phoebus' lodging! Such a wagoner
As Phaeton would whip you to the west
And bring in cloudy night immediately.
Spread thy close curtain, love-performing night,
That runaway's eyes may wink, and Romeo
Leap to these arms untalked of and unseen.
Lovers can see to do their amorous rites
By their own beauties; or, if love be blind,
It best agrees with night. Come, civil night,   10
Thou sober-suited matron, all in black,
And learn me how to lose a winning match,
Played for a pair of stainless maidenhoods.
Hood my unmanned blood, bating in my cheeks,
With thy black mantle till strange love grow bold,
Think true love acted simple modesty.
Come night, come Romeo, come thou day in night,
For thou wilt lie upon the wings of night
Whiter than new snow upon a raven's back.
Come gentle night, come loving black-browed night,   20
Give me my Romeo; and, when he shall die,
Take him and cut him out in little stars,
And he will make the face of heaven so fine
That all the world will be in love with night
And pay no worship to the garish sun.
O, I have bought the mansion of a love,
But not possessed it, and though I am sold,
Not yet enjoyed. So tedious is this day

1 – 4. Juliet, anxious to consummate her marriage with Romeo, wishes the day would pass quickly. In Greek mythology, Phoebus is the god of the sun.

9. *By their own beauties* – By the light of their own beauty
10. *civil* – solemn
12. *learn* – teach
12. *lose ... match* – a paradox; by surrendering or losing her virginity, she gains a husband

14 – 15. *Hood ... bold* – an image from falconry. A hood would be placed over an untrained (unmanned) hawk to calm it and to keep it from flapping its wings uncontrollably. Juliet is here admitting that she is somewhat out of control and would like the darkness of night to calm her till she is more used to love's processes.

25. *garish* – gaudy

RELATED READING

On Playing Juliet –
recollection by Peggy
Ashcroft (page 146)

As is the night before some festival
To an impatient child that hath new robes   30
And may not wear them. O, here comes my Nurse,

Enter Nurse, with cords.

And she brings news, and every tongue that speaks
But Romeo's name speaks heavenly eloquence.
Now, Nurse, what news? What hast thou there?
The cords that Romeo bid thee fetch?
NURSE: Ay, ay, the cords.
JULIET: Ay me, what news? Why dost thou wring thy hands?
NURSE: Ah, weraday, he's dead, he's dead, he's dead!
We are undone, lady, we are undone!
Alack the day, he's gone, he's killed, he's dead!   40
JULIET: Can heaven be so envious?
NURSE: Romeo can,
Though heaven cannot. O Romeo, Romeo,
Who ever would have thought it? Romeo!
JULIET: What devil art thou that dost torment me thus?
This torture should be roared in dismal hell.
Hath Romeo slain himself? Say thou but "Ay,"
And that bare vowel 'I' shall poison more
Than the death-darting eye of cockatrice.
I am not I, if there be such an 'I,'   50
Or those eyes shut that make thee answer "Ay."
If he be slain, say "Ay"; or if not, "No."
Brief sounds determine of my weal or woe.
NURSE: I saw the wound, I saw it with mine eyes —
God save the mark — here on his manly breast.
A piteous corse, a bloody piteous corse;
Pale, pale as ashes, all bedaubed in blood,
All in gore-blood. I swounded at the sight.
JULIET: O, break, my heart! Poor bankrupt, break at once!
To prison, eyes, never look on liberty.   60
Vile earth, to earth resign, end motion here,
And thou and Romeo press one heavy bier.
NURSE: O Tybalt, Tybalt, the best friend I had.
O courteous Tybalt, honest gentleman
That ever I should live to see thee dead.
JULIET: What storm is this that blows so contrary?
Is Romeo slaughtered, and is Tybalt dead?
My dearest cousin and my dearer lord?
Then, dreadful trumpet, sound the general doom,
For who is living if those two are gone?   70

38. *wereday* – welladay; alas
41. *envious* – jealous (of
Juliet's happiness) or full of
hatred

49. *cockatrice* – a monster
with the body of a serpent
and the head of a cock.
According to myth, it could
kill merely by looking at
someone.

cockatrice

53. *weal* – happiness;
well-being

69. *general doom* –
Doomsday

NURSE: Tybalt is gone and Romeo banished.
      Romeo that killed him, he is banished.
JULIET: O God! Did Romeo's hand shed Tybalt's blood?
NURSE: It did, it did, alas the day, it did!
JULIET: O serpent heart, hid with a flowering face!
      Did ever dragon keep so fair a cave?
      Beautiful tyrant, fiend angelical,
      Dove-feathered raven, wolvish-ravening lamb,
      Despised substance of divinest show!
      Just opposite to what thou justly seem'st —   80
      A damned saint, an honourable villain!
      O nature, what hadst thou to do in hell
      When thou didst bower the spirit of a fiend
      In mortal paradise of such sweet flesh?
      Was ever book containing such vile matter
      So fairly bound? O, that deceit should dwell
      In such a gorgeous palace!
NURSE: There's no trust,
      No faith, no honesty in men. All perjured,
      All forsworn, all naught, all dissemblers.   90
      Ah, where's my man? Give me some aqua vitae.
      These griefs, these woes, these sorrows make me old.
      Shame come to Romeo.
JULIET: Blistered be thy tongue
      For such a wish! He was not born to shame.
      Upon his brow shame is ashamed to sit,
      For 'tis a throne where honour may be crowned
      Sole monarch of the universal earth.
      O, what a beast was I to chide at him.
NURSE: Will you speak well of him that killed your cousin?   100
JULIET: Shall I speak ill of him that is my husband?
      Ah, poor my lord, what tongue shall smooth thy name
      When I, thy three-hours wife, have mangled it?
      But wherefore, villain, didst thou kill my cousin?
      That villain cousin would have killed my husband.
      Back, foolish tears, back to your native spring!
      Your tributary drops belong to woe,
      Which you, mistaking, offer up to joy.
      My husband lives, that Tybalt would have slain;
      And Tybalt's dead, that would have slain my husband.   110
      All this is comfort. Wherefore weep I then?
      Some word there was, worser than Tybalt's death,
      That murdered me. I would forget it fain,
      But O, it presses to my memory
      Like damned guilty deeds to sinners' minds.

75 – 87. Juliet employs a series of contrasting images (see note on *oxymoron* on page 19) to describe Romeo. These images serve to express the mixed emotions Juliet feels about Romeo, who is both her husband and the murderer of her dearest cousin.

83. *bower* – provide a home to

89 – 90. *All ... dissemblers* – The Nurse accuses men of being liars, oath-breakers, wicked persons, and deceivers.
91. *aqua vitae* – brandy

107 – 108. *Your ... joy* – Although Juliet is crying, her tears are not of sorrow but rather of joy because Romeo is still alive.

113. *fain* – gladly

Act Three • Scene 2

"Tybalt is dead and Romeo — banished."
That "banished," that one word "banished,"
Hath slain ten thousand Tybalts. Tybalt's death
Was woe enough, if it had ended there.
Or, if sour woe delights in fellowship   120
And needly will be ranked with other griefs,
Why followed not, when she said "Tybalt's dead,"
Thy father, or thy mother, nay or both,
Which modern lamentation might have moved?
But with a rearward following Tybalt's death,
"Romeo is banished" — to speak that word
Is father, mother, Tybalt, Romeo, Juliet,
All slain, all dead. Romeo is banished,
There is no end, no limit, measure, bound,
In that word's death. No words can that woe sound.   130
Where is my father and my mother, Nurse?

NURSE: Weeping and wailing over Tybalt's corse.
Will you go to them? I will bring you thither.

JULIET: Wash they his wounds with tears? Mine shall be spent,
When theirs are dry, for Romeo's banishment.
Take up those cords. Poor ropes, you are beguiled,
Both you and I, for Romeo is exiled.
He made you for a highway to my bed,
But I, a maid, die maiden-widowed.
Come, cords, come, Nurse, I'll to my wedding bed,   140
And death, not Romeo, take my maidenhead!

NURSE: Hie to your chamber. I'll find Romeo
To comfort you. I wot well where he is.
Hark ye, your Romeo will be here at night.
I'll to him. He is hid at Laurence' cell.

JULIET: O, find him, give this ring to my true knight
And bid him come to take his last farewell.

Exeunt.

121. *needly* – of necessity

124. *modern* – common, everyday
125. *rearward* – rearguard in an army, a final assault of griefs on Juliet

136. *beguiled* – cheated; deceived

143. *wot* – know

Act Three
Scene 3

Friar Laurence's cell.

Enter Friar [Laurence].

FRIAR: Romeo, come forth, come forth, thou fearful man.
Affliction is enamoured of thy parts,
And thou art wedded to calamity.

Enter Romeo.

ROMEO: Father, what news? What is the Prince's doom?
What sorrow craves acquaintance at my hand
That I yet know not?
FRIAR: Too familiar
Is my dear son with such sour company.
I bring thee tidings of the Prince's doom.
ROMEO: What less than doomsday is the Prince's doom?   10
FRIAR: A gentler judgment vanished from his lips:
Not body's death, but body's banishment.
ROMEO: Ha, banishment? Be merciful, say "death."
For exile hath more terror in his look,
Much more than death. Do not say "banishment."
FRIAR: Hence from Verona art thou banished.
Be patient, for the world is broad and wide.
ROMEO: There is no world without Verona walls,
But purgatory, torture, hell itself.
Hence "banished" is banished from the world,   20
And world's exile is death. Then "banished"
Is death mistermed. Calling death "banished,"
Thou cut'st my head off with a golden axe
And smilest upon the stroke that murders me.

Friar Laurence informs Romeo that the Prince has banished him from Verona for killing Tybalt. To Romeo, exile is worse than death, and he attempts to stab himself. The Friar calms Romeo and convinces him that his situation is not that desperate. With the Nurse's help, Romeo prepares to visit Juliet before leaving Verona.

1. *fearful* – full of fear
2 – 3. Friar Laurence suggests that bad luck seems so in love with Romeo that they are wedded to each other.

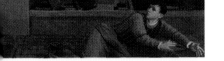

26. *Thy ... death* – Our law considers your crime as being punishable by death.
27. *rushed* – thrust; brushed

34. *validity* – value

46. *mean* – play on two meanings of "mean" – method and base

50. *divine* – priest

53. *fond* – foolish

64. *dispute* – discuss

FRIAR: O deadly sin! O rude unthankfulness!
     Thy fault our law calls death, but the kind Prince,
     Taking thy part, hath rushed aside the law,
     And turned that black word "death" to banishment.
     This is dear mercy, and thou seest it not.
ROMEO: 'Tis torture, and not mercy. Heaven is here   30
     Where Juliet lives, and every cat and dog
     And little mouse, every unworthy thing,
     Live here in heaven and may look on her,
     But Romeo may not. More validity,
     More honourable state, more courtship lives
     In carrion flies than Romeo. They may seize
     On the white wonder of dear Juliet's hand
     And steal immortal blessing from her lips,
     Who, even in pure and vestal modesty,
     Still blush, as thinking their own kisses sin.   40
     But Romeo may not, he is banished.
     Flies may do this, but I from this must fly.
     They are free men but I am banished.
     And sayest thou yet that exile is not death?
     Hadst thou no poison mixed, no sharp-ground knife,
     No sudden mean of death, though never so mean,
     But "banished" to kill me? "Banished"?
     O Friar, the damned use that word in hell.
     Howling attends it! How hast thou the heart,
     Being a divine, a ghostly confessor,   50
     A sin-absolver, and my friend professed,
     To mangle me with that word "banished"?
FRIAR: Thou fond mad man, hear me a little speak.
ROMEO: O, thou wilt speak again of banishment.
FRIAR: I'll give thee armour to keep off that word,
     Adversity's sweet milk, philosophy,
     To comfort thee, though thou art banished.
ROMEO: Yet "banished"? Hang up philosophy.
     Unless philosophy can make a Juliet,
     Displant a town, reverse a Prince's doom,   60
     It helps not, it prevails not. Talk no more.
FRIAR: O, then I see that madmen have no ears.
ROMEO: How should they, when that wise men have no eyes?
FRIAR: Let me dispute with thee of thy estate.
ROMEO: Thou canst not speak of that thou dost not feel.
     Wert thou as young as I, Juliet thy love,
     An hour but married, Tybalt murdered,
     Doting like me, and like me banished,

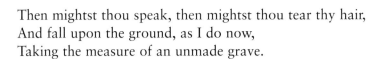

Then mightst thou speak, then mightst thou tear thy hair,
And fall upon the ground, as I do now,   70
Taking the measure of an unmade grave.

Knock within.

FRIAR: Arise, one knocks. Good Romeo, hide thyself.
ROMEO: Not I, unless the breath of heartsick groans
Mist-like infold me from the search of eyes.

Knock.

FRIAR: Hark, how they knock! Who's there? Romeo, arise,
Thou wilt be taken. — Stay awhile! — Stand up.

Knock.

Run to my study. — By and by! — God's will,
What simpleness is this. — I come, I come!

78. *simpleness* – foolishness

Knock.

Who knocks so hard? Whence come you? What's your will?
NURSE: *[Within.]* Let me come in, and you shall know my errand. 80
I come from Lady Juliet.
FRIAR: Welcome then.

Enter Nurse.

NURSE: O holy Friar, O, tell me, holy Friar,
Where is my lady's lord, where's Romeo?
FRIAR: There on the ground, with his own tears made drunk.
NURSE: O, he is even in my mistress' case,
Just in her case! O woeful sympathy!
Piteous predicament! Even so lies she,
Blubbering and weeping, weeping and blubbering.
Stand up, stand up. Stand, and you be a man.   90
For Juliet's sake, for her sake, rise and stand!
Why should you fall into so deep an O?
ROMEO: *[He rises.]* Nurse —
NURSE: Ah sir, ah sir. Well, death's the end of all.
ROMEO: Spakest thou of Juliet? How is it with her?
Doth not she think me an old murderer,

87. *woeful sympathy* – there is a similarity (harmony) in their grief

97. *childhood* – freshness, newness

100. *cancelled* – made null and void because the marriage has not been consummated

110. *sack* – attack; ransack

116. *seeming* – what would seem

116 – 117. "It would seem you are a man, but you act like a woman; you are more like a monstrous beast in seeming both a man and a woman."

Now I have stained the childhood of our joy
With blood removed but little from her own?
Where is she? And how doth she? And what says
My concealed lady to our cancelled love?   **100**

NURSE: O, she says nothing, sir, but weeps and weeps,
And now falls on her bed, and then starts up,
And Tybalt calls, and then on Romeo cries,
And then down falls again.

ROMEO: As if that name,
Shot from the deadly level of a gun,
Did murder her, as that name's cursed hand
Murdered her kinsman. O, tell me, Friar, tell me,
In what vile part of this anatomy
Doth my name lodge? Tell me, that I may sack   **110**
The hateful mansion.

[Draws his dagger and attempts to stab himself.]

FRIAR: Hold thy desperate hand.
Art thou a man? Thy form cries out thou art.
Thy tears are womanish, thy wild acts denote
The unreasonable fury of a beast.
Unseemly woman in a seeming man,
And ill-beseeming beast in seeming both!
Thou hast amazed me. By my holy order,
I thought thy disposition better tempered.

Hast thou slain Tybalt? Wilt thou slay thyself?   120
And slay thy lady that in thy life lives,
By doing damned hate upon thyself?
Why railest thou on thy birth, the heaven, and earth?
Since birth and heaven and earth, all three do meet
In thee at once, which thou at once wouldst lose.
Fie, fie, thou shamest thy shape, thy love, thy wit,
Which, like a usurer, abound'st in all,
And usest none in that true use indeed
Which should bedeck thy shape, thy love, thy wit.
Thy noble shape is but a form of wax   130
Digressing from the valour of a man.
Thy dear love sworn but hollow perjury,
Killing that love which thou hast vowed to cherish;
Thy wit, that ornament to shape and love,
Misshapen in the conduct of them both,
Like powder in a skilless soldier's flask,
Is set afire by thine own ignorance,
And thou dismembered with thine own defence.
What, rouse thee, man! Thy Juliet is alive,
For whose dear sake thou wast but lately dead.   140
There art thou happy. Tybalt would kill thee,
But thou slewest Tybalt. There art thou happy.
The law, that threatened death, becomes thy friend
And turns it to exile. There art thou happy.
A pack of blessings light upon thy back;

126. *wit* – intelligence
128 – 129. "Like a money lender who has abundance in all but does not use his wealth properly"
130 – 131. "Like a figure in wax, you have the form and shape of a man but not the substance because you lack courage."
136 – 138. Romeo's intelligence is like gunpowder in an inept soldier's flask that is set afire through ignorance. Romeo, by not using his intelligence, could be destroyed by that which should defend him.

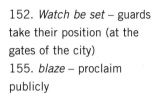

Happiness courts thee in her best array;
But, like a misbehaved and sullen wench,
Thou pouts upon thy fortune and thy love.
Take heed, take heed, for such die miserable.
Go get thee to thy love, as was decreed,   150
Ascend her chamber — hence and comfort her.

152. *Watch be set* – guards take their position (at the gates of the city)

But look thou stay not till the Watch be set,
For then thou canst not pass to Mantua,
Where thou shalt live till we can find a time

155. *blaze* – proclaim publicly

To blaze your marriage, reconcile your friends,
Beg pardon of the Prince, and call thee back
With twenty hundred thousand times more joy
Than thou wentst forth in lamentation.
Go before, Nurse. Commend me to thy lady
And bid her hasten all the house to bed,   160
Which heavy sorrow makes them apt unto.
Romeo is coming.

NURSE: O Lord, I could have stayed here all the night
To hear good counsel. O, what learning is.
My lord, I'll tell my lady you will come.

166. *chide* – scold

ROMEO: Do so, and bid my sweet prepare to chide.

Nurse offers to go in and turns again.

NURSE: Here sir, is a ring she bid me give you.
Hie you, make haste, for it grows very late.

Exit Nurse.

ROMEO: How well my comfort is revived by this.
FRIAR: Go hence, good night, and here stands all your state: 170
Either be gone before the Watch be set,
Or by the break of day disguised from hence.

173. *Sojourn* – stay
174. *signify* – let you know
175. *hap* – happening

Sojourn in Mantua. I'll find out your man,
And he shall signify from time to time
Every good hap to you that chances here.
Give me thy hand. 'Tis late. Farewell. Good night.
ROMEO: But that a joy past joy calls out on me,

178. *brief* – hastily

It were a grief so brief to part with thee.
Farewell.

Exeunt.

Act Three
Scene 4

Capulet's house.

It is late Monday night. Capulet and Paris discuss wedding arrangements and agree that the ceremony should take place in three days — on Thursday. Capulet asks his wife before she goes to bed to inform Juliet of their decision.

Enter Capulet, Lady Capulet, and Paris.

CAPULET: Things have fallen out, sir, so unluckily
That we have had no time to move our daughter.
Look you, she loved her kinsman Tybalt dearly,
And so did I. Well, we were born to die.
'Tis very late. She'll not come down tonight.
I promise you, but for your company,
I would have been abed an hour ago.
PARIS: These times of woe afford no times to woo.
Madam, good night. Commend me to your daughter.
LADY CAPULET: I will, and know her mind early tomorrow.   10
Tonight she's mewed up to her heaviness.

Paris offers to go in, and Capulet calls him again.

CAPULET: Sir Paris, I will make a desperate tender
Of my child's love. I think she will be ruled
In all respects by me — nay more, I doubt it not.
Wife, go you to her ere you go to bed,
Acquaint her here of my son Paris' love,
And bid her — mark you me? — on Wednesday next —
But, soft — what day is this?
PARIS: Monday, my lord.
CAPULET: Monday! Ha, ha! Well, Wednesday is too soon.   20
A Thursday let it be — a Thursday, tell her,
She shall be married to this noble earl.
Will you be ready? Do you like this haste?
We'll keep no great ado — a friend or two.
For hark you, Tybalt being slain so late,
It may be thought we held him carelessly,

2. *move* – persuade

11. *mewed up* – shut up
12. *tender* – offer

> "It has often been said that the play is in part about the hastiness of youth. I would say that it is in part about the hastiness of everyone, of the old as well as the young."
> – Bert Cardullo, professor, Yale University School of Drama

24. *keep … ado* – keep the wedding celebration small and simple
26. *carelessly* – without care; lightly

Being our kinsman, if we revel much.
Therefore we'll have some half a dozen friends
And there an end. But what say you to Thursday?

PARIS: My lord, I would that Thursday were tomorrow.   30

CAPULET: Well, get you gone. A Thursday be it then.
Go you to Juliet ere you go to bed,
Prepare her, wife, against this wedding day.
Farewell, my lord. — Light to my chamber, ho!
Afore me, it is so very very late that we
May call it early by and by. Good night.

Exeunt.

Act Three
Scene 5

Capulet's orchard.

Enter Romeo and Juliet aloft, at the window.

JULIET: Wilt thou be gone? It is not yet near day.
It was the nightingale and not the lark
That pierced the fearful hollow of thine ear.
Nightly she sings on yond pomegranate tree.
Believe me, love, it was the nightingale.

ROMEO: It was the lark, the herald of the morn,
No nightingale. Look, love, what envious streaks
Do lace the severing clouds in yonder east.
Night's candles are burnt out, and jocund day
Stands tiptoe on the misty mountain tops.　　　　　10
I must be gone and live, or stay and die.

JULIET: Yond light is not daylight, I know it, I.
It is some meteor that the sun exhales
To be to thee this night a torchbearer
And light thee on the way to Mantua.
Therefore stay yet. Thou need'st not to be gone.

ROMEO: Let me be taken, let me be put to death.
I am content, so thou wilt have it so.
I'll say yon grey is not the morning's eye,
'Tis but the pale reflex of Cynthia's brow.　　　　　20
Nor that is not the lark whose notes do beat
The vaulty heaven so high above our heads.
I have more care to stay than will to go.
Come, death, and welcome. Juliet wills it so.
How is it, my soul? Let's talk. It is not day.

JULIET: It is, it is. Hie hence, be gone, away.
It is the lark that sings so out of tune,
Straining harsh discords and unpleasing sharps.

It is early Tuesday morning. Romeo, having spent the night with Juliet, must leave Verona before he is caught by the Prince's men. As they part, both have premonitions foreboding death. Lady Capulet informs Juliet that she is to marry Paris on Thursday. When Juliet objects, her father tells her that if she does not succumb to his will, he will disown her. Later, the Nurse advises Juliet to forget Romeo and marry Paris. Juliet swears to never trust the Nurse again. She plans on visiting Friar Laurence immediately to see if he has a remedy for her dilemma.

2. *nightingale* – night songbird
2. *lark* – morning songbird
9. *Night's candles* – stars
9. *jocund* – cheerful

20. *Cynthia* – goddess of the moon

28. *sharps* – shrill high notes

29. *division* – rapid, musical notes that are distinct from each other

33. *affray* – frighten
34. *hunt's-up* – song to rouse hunters

The play *Romeo and Juliet:* "If it has the sweetness of the rose, it has its freshness too; if it has the languor of the nightingale's song, it has also its giddy transport; if it has the softness of a southern spring, it is as glowing and bright."
– William Hazlitt (1778 – 1830), British essayist and critic

54. *ill-divining soul* – a soul that foresees ruin or evil

55 – 59. Even the masterful Shakespeare can be guilty of overly obvious foreshadowing. In the dim light of dawn, the lovers both have premonitions and see each other as looking dead.

Fortune's wheel

Some say the lark makes sweet division.
This doth not so, for she divideth us.   30
Some say the lark and loathed toad change eyes.
O, now I would they had changed voices too,
Since arm from arm that voice doth us affray,
Hunting thee hence with hunt's-up to the day.
O, now be gone! More light and light it grows.
ROMEO: More light and light — more dark and dark our woes.

Enter Nurse hastily.

NURSE: Madam!
JULIET: Nurse?
NURSE: Your lady mother is coming to your chamber.
The day is broke, be wary, look about.   40

[Exit Nurse.]

JULIET: Then, window, let day in and let life out.
ROMEO: Farewell, farewell! One kiss, and I'll descend.

He goes down.

JULIET: Art thou gone so? Love, lord, ay husband, friend,
I must hear from thee every day in the hour,
For in a minute there are many days.
O, by this count I shall be much in years
Ere I again behold my Romeo.
ROMEO: Farewell!
I will omit no opportunity
That may convey my greetings, love, to thee.   50
JULIET: O, thinkest thou we shall ever meet again?
ROMEO: I doubt it not, and all these woes shall serve
For sweet discourses in our time to come.
JULIET: O God, I have an ill-divining soul!
Methinks I see thee, now thou art so low,
As one dead in the bottom of a tomb.
Either my eyesight fails, or thou lookest pale.
ROMEO: And trust me, love, in my eye so do you.
Dry sorrow drinks our blood. Adieu, adieu!

Exit.

JULIET: O Fortune, Fortune! All men call thee fickle.   60
If thou art fickle, what dost thou with him

That is renowned for faith? Be fickle, Fortune,
For then I hope thou wilt not keep him long
But send him back.

Enter Lady Capulet.

LADY CAPULET: Ho, daughter! are you up?
JULIET: Who is it that calls? It is my lady mother.
    Is she not down so late, or up so early?
    What unaccustomed cause procures her hither?

[Juliet] goeth down from the window.

LADY CAPULET: Why, how now, Juliet?

[Enter Juliet.]

JULIET: Madam, I am not well.   70
LADY CAPULET: Evermore weeping for your cousin's death?
    What, wilt thou wash him from his grave with tears?
    And if thou couldst, thou couldst not make him live.
    Therefore have done. Some grief shows much of love,
    But much of grief shows still some want of wit.
JULIET: Yet let me weep for such a feeling loss.
LADY CAPULET: So shall you feel the loss but not the friend
    Which you weep for.
JULIET: Feeling so the loss,
    I cannot choose but ever weep the friend.   80
LADY CAPULET: Well, girl, thou weepest not so much for his
      death
    As that the villain lives which slaughtered him.
JULIET: What villain, madam?
LADY CAPULET: That same villain Romeo.
JULIET: *[Aside.]* Villain and he be many miles asunder. —
    God pardon him! I do, with all my heart.
    And yet no man like he doth grieve my heart.
LADY CAPULET: That is because the traitor murderer lives.
JULIET: Ay, madam, from the reach of these my hands.
    Would none but I might venge my cousin's death.   90
LADY CAPULET: We will have vengeance for it, fear thou not.
    Then weep no more. I'll send to one in Mantua,
    Where that same banished runagate doth live,
    Shall give him such an unaccustomed dram
    That he shall soon keep Tybalt company,
    And then I hope thou wilt be satisfied.

68. "What is so out of the ordinary, that she comes here?"

76. *feeling* – heartfelt

90. Juliet's mother does not appreciate the irony in Juliet's words.

92. *Mantua* – How would Juliet's mother know so quickly of Romeo's whereabouts? He left just moments previous. This is not explained in the play.

94. *unaccustomed dram* – unexpected drink (of poison)

JULIET: Indeed I never shall be satisfied
 With Romeo till I behold him — dead —
 Is my poor heart so for a kinsman vexed.
 Madam, if you could find out but a man   100
 To bear a poison, I would temper it —
 That Romeo should, upon receipt thereof
 Soon sleep in quiet. O, how my heart abhors
 To hear him named, and cannot come to him
 To wreak the love I bore my cousin
 Upon his body that hath slaughtered him.
LADY CAPULET: Find thou the means and I'll find such a man.
 But now I'll tell thee joyful tidings, girl.
JULIET: And joy comes well in such a needy time.
 What are they, I beseech your ladyship?   110
LADY CAPULET: Well, well, thou hast a careful father, child,
 One who to put thee from thy heaviness,
 Hath sorted out a sudden day of joy
 That thou expects not nor I looked not for.
JULIET: Madam, in happy time! What day is that?
LADY CAPULET: Marry, my child, early next Thursday morn
 The gallant, young, and noble gentleman,
 The County Paris, at Saint Peter's Church,
 Shall happily make thee there a joyful bride.
JULIET: Now by Saint Peter's Church, and Peter too, 120
 He shall not make me there a joyful bride!
 I wonder at this haste, that I must wed
 Ere he that should be husband comes to woo.
 I pray you tell my lord and father, madam,
 I will not marry yet. And when I do, I swear
 It shall be Romeo, whom you know I hate,
 Rather than Paris. These are news indeed!
LADY CAPULET: Here comes your father. Tell him so yourself,
 And see how he will take it at your hands.

Enter Capulet and Nurse.

CAPULET: When the sun sets the air doth drizzle dew, 130
 But for the sunset of my brother's son
 It rains downright.
 How now, a conduit, girl? What, still in tears?
 Evermore showering? In one little body
 Thou counterfeits a bark, a sea, a wind.
 For still thy eyes, which I may call the sea,
 Do ebb and flow with tears. The bark thy body is,
 Sailing in this salt flood; the winds, thy sighs,

---

101. *temper* – mix; fix

111. *careful* – thoughtful, sensitive

131. *sunset of my brother's son* – death of Tybalt
133. *conduit* – water fountain created in the shape of a human
135. *counterfeits a bark* – projects the image of a boat

Act Three • Scene 5

Who, raging with thy tears and they with them,
Without a sudden calm will overset   140
Thy tempest-tossed body. How now, wife?
Have you delivered to her our decree?

LADY CAPULET: Ay, sir, but she will none, she gives you thanks.
I would the fool were married to her grave!

CAPULET: Soft! Take me with you, take me with you, wife.
How? Will she none? Doth she not give us thanks?
Is she not proud? Doth she not count her blest,
Unworthy as she is, that we have wrought
So worthy a gentleman to be her bridegroom?

JULIET: Not proud you have, but thankful that you have.   150
Proud can I never be of what I hate,
But thankful even for hate that is meant love.

CAPULET: How now, how now? Chopped logic? What is this?
"Proud" and "I thank you" and "I thank you not"
And yet "not proud"? Mistress minion you,
Thank me no thankings, nor proud me no prouds,
But fettle your fine joints 'gainst Thursday next
To go with Paris to Saint Peter's Church,
Or I will drag thee on a hurdle thither.
Out, you green-sickness carrion! Out, you baggage!   160
You tallow-face!

LADY CAPULET: Fie, fie! What, are you mad?

JULIET: Good father, I beseech you on my knees,

She kneels down.

Hear me with patience but to speak a word.

CAPULET: Hang thee, young baggage, disobedient wretch!
I tell thee what — get thee to church a Thursday
Or never after look me in the face.
Speak not, reply not, do not answer me!
My fingers itch. Wife, we scarce thought us blest
That God had lent us but this only child.   170
But now I see this one is one too much,
And that we have a curse in having her.
Out on her, hilding!

NURSE: God in heaven bless her.
You are to blame, my lord, to rate her so.

CAPULET: And why, my Lady Wisdom? Hold your tongue,
Good Prudence. Smatter with your gossips, go!

NURSE: I speak no treason.

CAPULET: O, God ye good even!

NURSE: May not one speak?   180

---

144. *I … grave* – Albeit a familiar phrase during the Elizabethan period, this is one wish that Lady Capulet will live to regret expressing.

150 – 152. "I am not proud but I am thankful. I cannot be happy with something I do not like, but I am grateful for what you've done because it proves that you love me."

155. *minion* – spoiled child

157. *fettle … joints* – get yourself ready

159. *hurdle* – the structure upon which traitors were tied and dragged to their place of execution

160. *green-sickness* – naive, immature

161. *tallow-face* – colourless and pale as candle wax

169. *My fingers itch* – Capulet is fighting the urge to strike his daughter.

173. *hilding* – worthless girl

177. *Smatter* – prattle; chatter

182. *gravity* – words of advice or wisdom

190. *demesnes* – domains; property

193. *puling* – whimpering
194. *mammet* – puppet, toy
194. *in ... tender* – who is fortunate in this offer

205. *be foresworn* – break my vow

CAPULET: Peace, you mumbling fool!
Utter your gravity over a gossip's bowl,
For here we need it not.
LADY CAPULET: You are too hot.
CAPULET: God's bread, it makes me mad!
Day, night, hour, tide time, work, play,
Alone, in company, still my care hath been
To have her matched. And having now provided
A gentleman of princely parentage,
Of fair demesnes, youthful, and nobly allied,   190
Stuffed, as they say, with honourable parts,
Proportioned as one's thought would wish a man —
And then to have a wretched puling fool,
A whining mammet, in her fortune's tender,
To answer "I'll not wed, I cannot love,
I am too young, I pray you pardon me!"
But, and you will not wed, I'll pardon you.
Graze where you will, you shall not house with me.
Look to it, think on it, I do not use to jest.
Thursday is near. Lay hand on heart. Advise.   200
And you be mine, I'll give you to my friend.
And you be not, hang, beg, starve, die in the streets.
For, by my soul, I'll never acknowledge thee,
Nor what is mine shall never do thee good.
Trust to it. Bethink you. I'll not be forsworn.

Exit.

JULIET: Is there no pity sitting in the clouds
That sees into the bottom of my grief?
O sweet my mother, cast me not away,
Delay this marriage for a month, a week,
Or if you do not, make the bridal bed   210
In that dim monument where Tybalt lies.
LADY CAPULET: Talk not to me, for I'll not speak a word.
Do as thou wilt, for I have done with thee.

Exit.

JULIET: O God, O nurse, how shall this be prevented?
My husband is on earth, my faith in heaven.
How shall that faith return again to earth
Unless that husband send it me from heaven
By leaving earth? Comfort me, counsel me.
Alack, alack, that heaven should practise stratagems

Upon so soft a subject as myself.   220
What sayst thou? Hast thou not a word of joy?
Some comfort, Nurse.

NURSE: Faith, here it is.
    Romeo is banished, and all the world to nothing
    That he dares never come back to challenge you.
    Or if he do, it needs must be by stealth.
    Then, since the case so stands as now it doth,
    I think it best you married with the County.
    O, he's a lovely gentleman.
    Romeo's a dishclout to him. An eagle, madam,   230
    Hath not so green, so quick, so fair an eye
    As Paris hath. Beshrew my very heart,
    I think you are happy in this second match,
    For it excels your first, or, if it did not,
    Your first is dead, or 'twere as good he were
    As living here and you no use of him.

JULIET: Speakest thou this from thy heart?

NURSE: And from my soul too, else beshrew them both.

JULIET: Amen!

NURSE: What?   240

JULIET: Well, thou hast comforted me marvellous much.
    Go in, and tell my lady I am gone,
    Having displeased my father, to Laurence' cell,
    To make confession and to be absolved.

NURSE: Marry, I will, and this is wisely done.

Exit.

JULIET: Ancient damnation! O most wicked fiend!
    Is it more sin to wish me thus forsworn,
    Or to dispraise my lord with that same tongue
    Which she hath praised him with above compare
    So many thousand times? Go, counsellor!   250
    Thou and my bosom henceforth shall be twain.
    I'll to the Friar to know his remedy.
    If all else fail, myself have power to die.

Exit.

∾ ∾ ∾

224. *all ... nothing* – The Nurse is willing to wager the whole world that Romeo will not return.

230. *dishclout* – dishcloth; rag

239. This marks the end of the relationship between Juliet and her Nurse. From here on, Juliet cannot depend on the Nurse for help or advice.

246. *Ancient damnation* – old, damnable woman

251. *twain* – apart

Act Three Considerations

ACT THREE Scene 1

▶ From what you have seen so far of Benvolio in this play, do you agree with Mercutio's characterization of him in lines 5 to 27? How much truth do you think there is in Mercutio's accounting of Benvolio?

▶ On line 140, Benvolio begins to tell his version of how Mercutio and Tybalt were killed. Is his a fair accounting of what happened? To what extent has Benvolio told the truth? Where does his story vary from what actually happened?

▶ Write obituaries for Mercutio and Tybalt. Find quotations from this scene (or others) that would serve as fitting epitaphs for their tombstones?

▶ Up to this point, things have gone rather well for Romeo and Juliet. This scene, however, marks the climax or turning point in the play. From here on, the fortunes of Romeo and Juliet will begin to decline.

Why exactly does Romeo kill Tybalt? Was it fate or his destiny to do so? Was it because of the feud? Or was it because of Romeo's basic character?

ACT THREE Scene 2

▶ The purpose of a soliloquy is to reveal to the audience what is going on in the mind and heart of the speaker. Sometimes soliloquies tell us about the speaker's motivation or plans. What does Juliet's soliloquy at the beginning of this scene reveal about her feelings and state of mind?

▶ In lines 75 to 87, Juliet uses a series of oxymorons to express the mixed emotions she feels towards Romeo. What are these emotions? Draw a chart containing two columns. In one column, place the words that express Juliet's positive feelings towards Romeo. In the other, place the words with the negative associations.

If you were asked to rewrite the play in modern-day language, what would this speech sound like? Rewrite the speech using a more contemporary series of contrasting terms.

▶ Despite her mixed emotions, Juliet is quite clear as to how she feels about her husband. If you were Juliet and writing a marriage manual, what basic rules would you formulate based on what Juliet says in the second half of this scene?

ACT THREE Scene 3

▶ Romeo accuses the Friar of being blind and incapable of knowing how Romeo feels. What arguments does Romeo use to support this view? Do you agree with Romeo's opinion in this matter?

- In this and the previous scene, the two lovers receive news of Romeo's fate. Who do you think acts more maturely in receiving the news? Explain.
- At the end of his long speech, the Friar outlines his plan for making all things right. What specifically is his plan? For it to succeed, the lovers and he will need some good luck. What kinds of things could go wrong?
- Part of the Friar's plan is to "beg pardon of the Prince." Imagine that you are the Friar. Write a letter or speech to the Prince in which you plead forgiveness for Romeo.

ACT THREE Scene 4

- In this scene it appears that Capulet has changed his mind about Juliet's being too young to marry. What do you think has caused this change? Write a short dialogue between Capulet and his wife in which they discuss whether or not they should give Paris permission to marry Juliet.
- What clues are there in this scene that suggest Capulet is the kind of person who is used to getting what he wants? What evidence is there in previous scenes that this may be the case?

ACT THREE Scene 5

- In the first sixty lines of this scene, as Romeo and Juliet take their leave of each other, they make numerous references to images of light and darkness. Make lists of the various images. What conclusions can you draw based on the use of such images?
- The scene between Juliet and her mother in which they discuss killing Romeo contains many examples of irony. Some say too much irony. What do you think? Does Shakespeare overdo it in this scene? What purpose is served by having Juliet and her mother discuss Romeo?
- At the beginning of the play Juliet is characterized as an obedient child. In what ways has Juliet changed?
- What does Capulet threaten to do if Juliet refuses to marry Paris? Would these threats be as effective today as they were four hundred years ago? Why or why not?
- By the end of the scene, Juliet finds herself completely isolated. There is no one (besides the Friar) to whom she can turn for help. Imagine that Juliet kept a diary. Write a short entry outlining how she now feels about her parents and the Nurse.

Act Four
Scene 1

Friar Laurence's cell.

Enter Friar Laurence and County Paris.

FRIAR: On Thursday, sir? The time is very short.
PARIS: My father Capulet will have it so,
   And I am nothing slow to slack his haste.
FRIAR: You say you do not know the lady's mind.
   Uneven is the course. I like it not.
PARIS: Immoderately she weeps for Tybalt's death,
   And therefore have I little talked of love,
   For Venus smiles not in a house of tears.
   Now, sir, her father counts it dangerous
   That she do give her sorrow so much sway,   10
   And in his wisdom hastes our marriage
   To stop the inundation of her tears
   Which, too much minded by herself alone,
   May be put from her by society.
   Now do you know the reason of this haste.
FRIAR: *[Aside.]* I would I knew not why it should be slowed. —
   Look, sir, here comes the lady toward my cell.

Enter Juliet.

PARIS: Happily met, my lady and my wife.
JULIET: That may be, sir, when I may be a wife.
PARIS: That may be, must be, love, on Thursday next.   20
JULIET: What must be shall be.
FRIAR: That's a certain text.
PARIS: Come you to make confession to this father?
JULIET: To answer that, I should confess to you.

Paris and Friar Laurence discuss the reasons for the hasty wedding. A desperate and distraught Juliet arrives to confer with the Friar. Once Paris departs, Friar Laurence suggests a plan that involves Juliet's taking a potion that will make it seem as if she were dead. The effects of the drug will last for forty-two hours. The family, believing Juliet to be dead, will take her to the Capulet burial vault. Romeo, the Friar elaborates, will be informed of the plan by letter and will arrive just before she awakes. The two of them will then escape to Mantua.

3. "I am in no way reluctant to slow him down."

5. *uneven* – irregular

12. *inundation* – flood; wave

13 – 14. According to Paris, the hasty marriage has been arranged to stop Juliet's flood of tears, which flow freely because she is alone (unmarried) but which may stop if she has companionship (a husband).

28. *price* – value

32. *it* – her face. Juliet declines to accept Paris's compliment, and suggests that her face was unattractive before it was ravaged with tears.

40. *pensive* – full of worries, sad
42. *shield* – forbid

48. *compass ... wits* – ability of my intelligence
49. *prorogue* – postpone; delay

58. *label ... deed* – Juliet is already legally married to Romeo. She will not tolerate a cancellation (label) of that bond through marriage to another.
63. *extremes* – impossible situation
64. *umpire* – judge
65. *commission* – authority, wisdom

PARIS: Do not deny to him that you love me.
JULIET: I will confess to you that I love him.
PARIS: So will ye, I am sure, that you love me.
JULIET: If I do so, it will be of more price,
  Being spoke behind your back, than to your face.
PARIS: Poor soul, thy face is much abused with tears.   30
JULIET: The tears have got small victory by that,
  For it was bad enough before their spite.
PARIS: Thou wrongest it more than tears with that report.
JULIET: That is no slander, sir, which is a truth,
  And what I spake, I spake it to my face.
PARIS: Thy face is mine, and thou hast slandered it.
JULIET: It may be so, for it is not mine own. —
  Are you at leisure, holy father, now,
  Or shall I come to you at evening mass?
FRIAR: My leisure serves me, pensive daughter, now.   40
  My lord, we must entreat the time alone.
PARIS: God shield I should disturb devotion.
  Juliet, on Thursday early will I rouse ye.
  Till then, adieu, and keep this holy kiss.

Exit.

JULIET: O, shut the door, and when thou hast done so,
  Come weep with me, past hope, past cure, past help!
FRIAR: Ah, Juliet, I already know thy grief.
  It strains me past the compass of my wits.
  I hear thou must — and nothing may prorogue it —
  On Thursday next be married to this County.   50
JULIET: Tell me not, Friar, that thou hearest of this,
  Unless thou tell me how I may prevent it.
  If in thy wisdom thou canst give no help,
  Do thou but call my resolution wise,
  And with this knife I'll help it presently.
  God joined my heart and Romeo's, thou our hands.
  And ere this hand, by thee to Romeo's sealed,
  Shall be the label to another deed,
  Or my true heart with treacherous revolt
  Turn to another, this shall slay them both.   60
  Therefore, out of thy long-experienced time,
  Give me some present counsel, or, behold:
  'Twixt my extremes and me this bloody knife
  Shall play the umpire, arbitrating that
  Which the commission of thy years and art
  Could to no issue of true honour bring.

Be not so long to speak. I long to die
If what thou speakest speak not of remedy.

Friar: Hold, daughter. I do spy a kind of hope,
Which craves as desperate an execution   70
As that is desperate which we would prevent.
If, rather than to marry County Paris,
Thou hast the strength of will to slay thyself,
Then is it likely thou wilt undertake
A thing like death to chide away this shame,
That cop'st with death himself to 'scape from it;
And, if thou darest, I'll give thee remedy.

Juliet: O, bid me leap, rather than marry Paris,
From off the battlements of any tower,
Or walk in thievish ways, or bid me lurk   80
Where serpents are. Chain me with roaring bears,
Or hide me nightly in a charnel house,
Overcovered quite with dead men's rattling bones,
With reeky shanks and yellow chapless skulls.
Or bid me go into a new-made grave
And hide me with a dead man in his shroud —
Things that, to hear them told, have made me tremble —
And I will do it without fear or doubt,
To live an unstained wife to my sweet love.

Friar: Hold, then. Go home, be merry, give consent   90
To marry Paris. Wednesday is tomorrow.
Tomorrow night look that thou lie alone.
Let not the Nurse lie with thee in thy chamber.
Take thou this vial, being then in bed,
And this distilling liquor drink thou off.
When presently through all thy veins shall run
A cold and drowsy humour, for no pulse
Shall keep his native progress, but surcease.
No warmth, no breath, shall testify thou livest,
The roses in thy lips and cheeks shall fade   100
To many ashes, thy eyes' windows fall
Like death when he shuts up the day of life.
Each part, deprived of supple government
Shall stiff and stark and cold appear, like death,
And in this borrowed likeness of shrunk death
Thou shalt continue two and forty hours,
And then awake as from a pleasant sleep.
Now, when the bridegroom in the morning comes
To rouse thee from thy bed, there art thou, dead.
Then, as the manner of our country is,   110
In thy best robes, uncovered on the bier

"Tragedy requires a situation where no solution is possible."
– W.B. Yeats (1865 – 1939), Irish poet and playwright

75. *chide* – scold
76. "That would require facing death in order to escape from it."

82. *charnel house* – It was not uncommon for burial plots to be recycled. When a new grave was required, an old one would be dug up, and the skulls and bones that were found during the digging would be placed in a small building attached to the church called the "charnel house."

84. *reeky shanks* – foul-smelling limbs

95. *distilling* – coursing through the body; distilled
97. *cold ... humour* – a fluid that will make you cold and drowsy
98. *native progress* – natural rhythm
98. *but surcease* – but it will seem to stop
101. *eyes' windows* – eyelids
103. *supple government* – power to move

114. *against* – before the time

120. *inconstant toy* – whim, foolish thought
121. *Abate* – weaken

126. *help afford* – offer help

Thou shalt be borne to that same ancient vault
Where all the kindred of the Capulets lie.
In the mean time, against thou shalt awake,
Shall Romeo by my letters know our drift
And hither shall he come, and he and I
Will watch thy waking, and that very night
Shall Romeo bear thee hence to Mantua.
And this shall free thee from this present shame,
If no inconstant toy nor womanish fear   120
Abate thy valour in the acting it.

JULIET: Give me, give me! O, tell not me of fear!

FRIAR: Hold! Get you gone. Be strong and prosperous
In this resolve. I'll send a friar with speed
To Mantua, with my letters to thy lord.

JULIET: Love give me strength, and strength shall help afford.
Farewell, dear father.

Exeunt.

Act Four
Scene 2

Capulet's house.

Enter Capulet, Lady Capulet, Nurse, and two or three Servingmen.

CAPULET: So many guests invite as here are writ.

[Exit a Servingman.]

Sirrah, go hire me twenty cunning cooks.
SERVANT: You shall have none ill, sir, for I'll try if they can lick their fingers.
CAPULET: How! Canst thou try them so?
SERVANT: Marry, sir, 'tis an ill cook that cannot lick his own fingers. Therefore he that cannot lick his fingers goes not with me.
CAPULET: Go, be gone.

Exit Servingman.

We shall be much unfurnished for this time.   10
What, is my daughter gone to Friar Laurence?
NURSE: Ay, forsooth.
CAPULET: Well, he may chance to do some good on her.
A peevish self-willed harlotry it is.

Enter Juliet.

NURSE: See where she comes from shrift with merry look.
CAPULET: How now, my headstrong? Where have you been gadding?
JULIET: Where I have learnt me to repent the sin

Capulet, confident that Juliet will agree to marry Paris, continues to prepare for the wedding feast. When Juliet returns from seeing Friar Laurence, she asks her father to forgive her sin of disobedience. An ecstatic Capulet decides the wedding should take place the very next day, Wednesday. Juliet retires to her room, accompanied by her Nurse, to prepare herself. Capulet plans to stay up all night to prepare for the wedding.

2. *twenty cunning cooks* – cunning means skilled. One has to wonder what happened to Capulet's plan to invite a half-dozen or so family members to attend the wedding.

5. *try* – test
6 – 7. An old proverb held that only a poor cook would be reluctant to lick his fingers.

10. *unfurnished* – unprepared

14. *peevish ... harlotry* – stubborn, willful good-for-nothing

19. *behests* – requests
19. *enjoined* – instructed

Of disobedient opposition
To you and your behests, and am enjoined
By holy Laurence to fall prostrate here   20
To beg your pardon. Pardon, I beseech you.
Henceforward I am ever ruled by you.

[She kneels down.]

CAPULET: Send for the County. Go tell him of this.
  I'll have this knot knit up tomorrow morning.
JULIET: I met the youthful lord at Laurence' cell,

26. *becomed* – fitting, appropriate

  And gave him what becomed love I might,
  Not stepping over the bounds of modesty.
CAPULET: Why, I am glad on it. This is well. Stand up.
  This is as it should be. Let me see the County.
  Ay, marry. Go, I say, and fetch him hither.   30
  Now, afore God, this reverend holy Friar,
  All our whole city is much bound to him.

33. *closet* – room

JULIET: Nurse, will you go with me into my closet
  To help me sort such needful ornaments
  As you think fit to furnish me tomorrow?
LADY CAPULET: No, not till Thursday. There is time enough.
CAPULET: Go, Nurse, go with her. We'll to church tomorrow.

Exeunt Juliet and Nurse.

LADY CAPULET: We shall be short in our provision.
  'Tis now near night.

40. *stir about* – stay up

CAPULET: Tush, I will stir about,   40
  And all things shall be well, I warrant thee, wife.

42. *deck* – dress

  Go thou to Juliet, help to deck up her.
  I'll not to bed tonight, let me alone.
  I'll play the housewife for this once. — What, ho! —

45. *forth* – out

  They are all forth. Well, I will walk myself
  To County Paris, to prepare him up
  Against tomorrow. My heart is wondrous light
  Since this same wayward girl is so reclaimed.

Exeunt.

Act Four
Scene 3

Juliet's chamber.

It is late Tuesday evening and Juliet dismisses her mother and the Nurse. Once alone, she debates whether or not she should take the vial provided to her by Friar Laurence. Despite her fears and uncertainties, she remembers her resolve and drinks the potion.

Enter Juliet and Nurse.

JULIET: Ay, those attires are best. But, gentle Nurse,
    I pray thee leave me to myself tonight,
    For I have need of many orisons
    To move the heavens to smile upon my state,
    Which, well thou knowest, is cross and full of sin.

3. *orisons* – prayers

5. *cross* – full of difficulties

Enter Lady Capulet.

LADY CAPULET: What, are you busy, ho? Need you my help?
JULIET: No, madam, we have culled such necessaries
    As are behoveful for our state tomorrow.
    So please you, let me now be left alone
    And let the Nurse this night sit up with you,   10
    For I am sure you have your hands full all
    In this so sudden business.
LADY CAPULET: Good night.
    Get thee to bed, and rest, for thou hast need.

7. *culled* – chosen
8. *behoveful* – fitting

Exeunt [Lady Capulet and Nurse].

JULIET: Farewell! God knows when we shall meet again.
    I have a faint cold fear thrills through my veins
    That almost freezes up the heat of life.
    I'll call them back again to comfort me.
    — Nurse! — What should she do here?
    My dismal scene I needs must act alone.   20

16. *thrills* – that trembles

Come, vial.
What if this mixture do not work at all?
Shall I be married then tomorrow morning?
No, no! This shall forbid it. Lie thou there.

[She lays down a dagger.]

What if it be a poison which the Friar
Subtly hath ministered to have me dead,
Lest in this marriage he should be dishonoured,
Because he married me before to Romeo?
I fear it is. And yet methinks it should not,
For he hath still been tried a holy man.   30
How if, when I am laid into the tomb,
I wake before the time that Romeo
Come to redeem me? There's a fearful point!
Shall I not then be stifled in the vault,
To whose foul mouth no healthsome air breathes in,
And there die strangled ere my Romeo comes?
Or, if I live, is it not very like
The horrible conceit of death and night,
Together with the terror of the place,

30. *still ... tried* – has always proven himself

38. *conceit* – thought; image

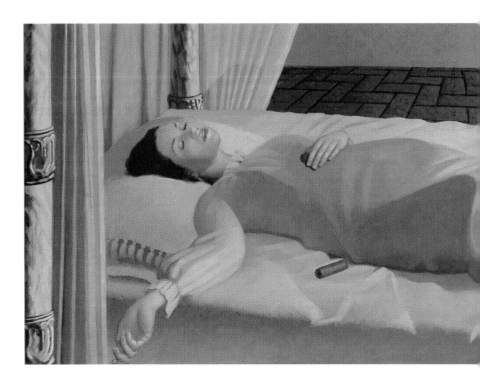

As in a vault, an ancient receptacle   40
Where for this many hundred years the bones
Of all my buried ancestors are packed,
Where bloody Tybalt, yet but green in earth,
Lies festering in his shroud, where, as they say,
At some hours in the night spirits resort —
Alack, alack! Is it not like that I
So early waking, what with loathsome smells,
And shrieks like mandrakes torn out of the earth,
That living mortals, hearing them, run mad —
O, if I wake, shall I not be distraught,   50
Environed with all these hideous fears,
And madly play with my forefathers' joints,
And pluck the mangled Tybalt from his shroud,
And, in this rage, with some great kinsman's bone
As with a club dash out my desperate brains?
O, look, methinks I see my cousin's ghost
Seeking out Romeo, that did spit his body
Upon a rapier's point. Stay, Tybalt, stay!
Romeo, Romeo, Romeo, here's drink! I drink to thee.

She falls upon her bed within the curtain.

48. *mandrakes* – plants whose roots resemble the human form. Popular superstition held that mandrakes shrieked when pulled from the earth.

mandrake

51. *Environed* – surrounded
52. *madly* – driven mad (by the horrors)

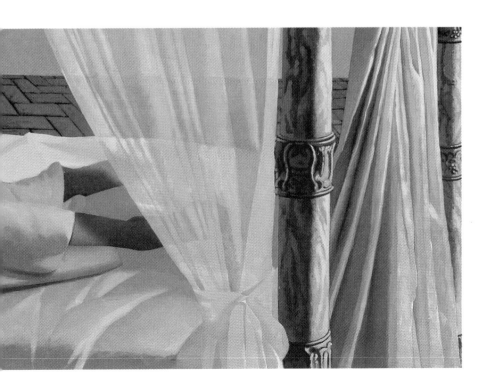

It is early Wednesday morning, and preparations are still underway for the upcoming wedding celebration. Capulet, upon hearing that Paris has arrived, orders that Juliet be awakened and dressed for the wedding.

5. *Angelica* – the Nurse's proper name. No reason is given for why Shakespeare provides the Nurse with this name at this particular time. This name is not used in any of the play's sources and is entirely Shakespeare's invention.

7. *cot-quean* – man who gets in the way by performing tasks that are usually the domain of domestic servants
10 – 11. *watched ... night* – stayed up all night before
12. *mouse-hunt* – prowler (after women)
13. *watch* – prevent by keeping her eye on him
14. *hood* – wife

Act Four
Scene 4

Capulet's house.

Enter Lady Capulet and Nurse.

LADY CAPULET: Hold, take these keys and fetch more spices,
        Nurse.
NURSE: They call for dates and quinces in the pastry.

Enter Capulet.

CAPULET: Come, stir, stir, stir! The second cock hath crowed,
        The curfew bell hath rung, 'tis three o'clock.
        Look to the baked meats, good Angelica.
        Spare not for cost.
NURSE: Go, you cot-quean, go,
        Get you to bed! Faith, you'll be sick tomorrow
        For this night's watching.
CAPULET: No, not a whit. What, I have watched ere now   10
        All night for lesser cause, and never been sick.
LADY CAPULET: Ay, you have been a mouse-hunt in your time;
        But I will watch you from such watching now.

Exeunt Lady Capulet and Nurse.

CAPULET: A jealous hood, a jealous hood!

Enter three or four Servants with spits and logs and baskets.

        Now, fellow, what is there?
1 SERVANT: Things for the cook, sir, but I know not what.

CAPULET: Make haste, make haste.

[Exit First Servant.]

Sirrah, fetch drier logs.
Call Peter, he will show thee where they are.
2 SERVANT: I have a head, sir, that will find out logs   20
And never trouble Peter for the matter.
CAPULET: Mass, and well said. A merry whoreson, ha.
Thou shalt be loggerhead.

[Exit Second Servant.]

Good faith, 'tis day.

Play music.

The County will be here with music straight,
For so he said he would. I hear him near.
Nurse! Wife! What, ho! What, Nurse, I say!

Enter Nurse.

Go waken Juliet, go and trim her up.
I'll go and chat with Paris. Hie, make haste,
Make haste! The bridegroom he is come already: 30
Make haste, I say.

[Exeunt.]

"The setting is Italian, some of the names are Italian but many are English. The action takes place during a hot Italian summer, late June. Yet the weather is more typical of England when Capulet asks for more logs for the fire."
– Cedric Watts, Shakespearean scholar and critic

22. *Mass* – mild oath, "By the Mass"
23. *loggerhead* – blockhead, with a pun on the current topic of discussion, logs

28. *trim* – dress

The Nurse discovers Juliet's seemingly lifeless body. The Capulets and Paris express their grief at the death of Juliet. When Friar Laurence arrives, he instructs them to prepare Juliet for her funeral.

Act Four
Scene 5

Juliet's chamber.

[Enter Nurse.]

1. *Fast* – fast asleep
2. *slug-abed* – lazy person

4. *pennyworths* – money's worth (of sleep)

NURSE: Mistress! What, mistress! Juliet! Fast, I warrant her, she.
Why, lamb, why, lady, fie. You slug-abed!
Why, love I say! Madam! Sweetheart! Why, bride!
What, not a word? You take your pennyworths now!
Sleep for a week, for the next night, I warrant,
The County Paris hath set up his rest
That you shall rest but little. God forgive me!
Marry and amen. How sound is she asleep!
I needs must wake her. Madam, madam, madam!
Ay, let the County take you in your bed!   10
He'll fright you up, in faith. Will it not be?

[Draws aside the curtains.]

What, dressed, and in your clothes, and down again?
I must needs wake you. Lady! Lady! Lady!
Alas, alas! Help, help! My lady's dead!

15. *weraday* – alas

O weraday that ever I was born!
Some aqua-vitae, ho! My lord! My lady!

Enter Lady Capulet.

LADY CAPULET: What noise is here?
NURSE: O lamentable day!
LADY CAPULET: What is the matter?
NURSE: Look, look! O heavy day!   20

LADY CAPULET: O me, O me! My child, my only life!
    Revive, look up, or I will die with thee!
    Help, help! Call help.

Enter Capulet.

CAPULET: For shame, bring Juliet forth. Her lord is come.
NURSE: She's dead, deceased! She's dead! Alack the day!
LADY CAPULET: Alack the day! She's dead, she's dead, she's
    dead!
CAPULET: Ha! Let me see her. Out alas. She's cold,
    Her blood is settled, and her joints are stiff.
    Life and these lips have long been separated.
    Death lies on her like an untimely frost   30
    Upon the sweetest flower of all the field.
NURSE: O lamentable day!
LADY CAPULET: O woeful time!
CAPULET: Death, that hath taken her hence to make me wail,
    Ties up my tongue and will not let me speak.

Enter Friar [Laurence] and Paris, and Musicians.

FRIAR: Come, is the bride ready to go to church?
CAPULET: Ready to go, but never to return.
    O son, the night before thy wedding day
    Hath Death lain with thy wife. See, there she lies,
    Flower as she was, deflowered by him.   40
    Death is my son-in-law, Death is my heir.
    My daughter he hath wedded. I will die,
    And leave him all. Life, living, all is Death's.
PARIS: Have I thought long to see this morning's face,
    And doth it give me such a sight as this?
LADY CAPULET: Accursed, unhappy, wretched, hateful day!
    Most miserable hour that ever Time saw
    In lasting labour of his pilgrimage!
    But one, poor one, one poor and loving child,
    But one thing to rejoice and solace in,   50
    And cruel Death hath catched it from my sight!
NURSE: O woe? O woeful, woeful, woeful day!
    Most lamentable day, most woeful day
    That ever, ever I did yet behold!
    O day! O day! O day! O hateful day!
    Never was seen so black a day as this.
    O woeful day! O woeful day!

30. *untimely* – early, unexpected

43. *living* – wealth, property

47 – 48. "This is the most miserable hour that Time has ever laboured through in his never-ending journey."

58. *Beguiled* – cheated

70. *Had part in* – shared

74. *promotion* – advancement in terms of wealth, happiness, and, ultimately, heaven

82. *rosemary* – herb, symbolic of remembrance
83. *corse* – corpse
84. *array* – clothing
85. *fond nature* – foolish human nature
86. "Human nature bids us weep but reason bids us be joyful (because Juliet is in heaven)."
87. *ordained* – intended to be

97. *lour* – frown
98. *Move* – anger

PARIS: Beguiled, divorced, wronged, spited, slain!
Most detestable Death, by thee beguiled,
By cruel, cruel thee quite overthrown!   60
O love! O life! Not life, but love in death.
CAPULET: Despised, distressed, hated, martyred, killed!
Uncomfortable time, why camest thou now
To murder, murder our solemnity?
O child! O child! My soul and not my child,
Dead art thou. Alack, my child is dead,
And with my child my joys are buried.
FRIAR: Peace, ho, for shame. Confusion's cure lives not
In these confusions. Heaven and yourself
Had part in this fair maid, now heaven hath all,   70
And all the better is it for the maid.
Your part in her you could not keep from death,
But heaven keeps his part in eternal life.
The most you sought was her promotion,
For 'twas your heaven she should be advanced,
And weep ye now, seeing she is advanced
Above the clouds, as high as heaven itself?
O, in this love, you love your child so ill
That you run mad, seeing that she is well.
She's not well married that lives married long,   80
But she's best married that dies married young.
Dry up your tears and stick your rosemary
On this fair corse, and, as the custom is,
And in her best array bear her to church.
For though fond nature bids us all lament,
Yet nature's tears are reason's merriment.
CAPULET: All things that we ordained festival
Turn from their office to black funeral.
Our instruments to melancholy bells,
Our wedding cheer to a sad burial feast;   90
Our solemn hymns to sullen dirges change,
Our bridal flowers serve for a buried corse,
And all things change them to the contrary.
FRIAR: Sir, go you in, and, madam, go with him,
And go, Sir Paris. Every one prepare
To follow this fair corse unto her grave.
The heavens do lour upon you for some ill.
Move them no more by crossing their high will.

*Exeunt all but Musicians and Nurse, casting rosemary
on her and shutting the curtains.*

1 MUSICIAN: Faith, we may put up our pipes and be gone.

NURSE: Honest good fellows, ah, put up, put up, For well you know this is a pitiful case. 100

1 MUSICIAN: Ay, by my troth, the case may be amended.

Exit Nurse.
Enter Peter.

PETER: Musicians, O, musicians, "Heart's ease," "Heart's ease"! O, and you will have me live, play "Heart's ease."

1 MUSICIAN: Why "Heart's ease"?

PETER: O, musicians, because my heart itself plays "My heart is full." O, play me some merry dump to comfort me.

1 MUSICIAN: Not a dump we! 'Tis no time to play now.

PETER: You will not then?

1 MUSICIAN: No. 110

PETER: I will then give it you soundly.

1 MUSICIAN: What will you give us?

PETER: No money, on my faith, but the gleek. I will give you the minstrel.

1 MUSICIAN: Then will I give you the serving-creature.

PETER: Then will I lay the serving-creature's dagger on your pate. I will carry no crotchets. I'll *re* you, I'll *fa* you. Do you note me?

1 MUSICIAN: And you *re* us and *fa* us, you note us.

2 MUSICIAN: Pray you put up your dagger, and put out your wit. 120

PETER: Then have at you with my wit! I will dry-beat you with an iron wit, and put up my iron dagger. Answer me like men.

"When griping grief the heart doth wound,
And doleful dumps the mind oppress,
Then music with her silver sound" —

Why "silver sound"? Why "music with her silver sound"? What say you, Simon Catling?

1 MUSICIAN: Marry, sir, because silver hath a sweet sound.

PETER: Prates! What say you, Hugh Rebeck?

2 MUSICIAN: I say "silver sound" because musicians sound for silver. 130

PETER: Prates too! What say you, James Soundpost?

3 MUSICIAN: Faith, I know not what to say.

PETER: O, I cry you mercy, you are the singer. I will say for you. It is "music with her silver sound" because musicians have no gold for sounding.

---

99. *put up* – pack up

102. *case ... amended* – This situation can be improved, or the case for my musical instrument can be mended.

103. *Heart's ease* – title of a popular song

107. *merry dump* – an oxymoron (dump refers to a sad song)

113. *gleek* – jest, scorn

114. *minstrel* – a term of contempt. Many minstrels were vagabonds and beggars.

115. "Then I will call you a common servant."
117. *pate* – head
117. *carry ... crotchets* – put up with any of your whims
117. *re ... fa* – musical notes
121. *dry-beat* – thrash

127. *Catling* – catgut used for a lute string
130. *sound for silver* – play for pay
131. *Prates* – he chatters
135. *no ... sounding* – the word *sounding* means at least two things – playing or testing. In either case, the point is being made that musicians (artists in general) lack gold and are poor.

137. *lend redress* – compensate

139 – 140. *tarry ... dinner* – wait for the mourners and stay for dinner

"Then music with her silver sound
With speedy help doth lend redress."

Exit.

1 MUSICIAN: What a pestilent knave is this same?
2 MUSICIAN: Hang him, Jack! Come, we'll in here, tarry for the mourners, and stay dinner.

Exeunt.

❧ ❧ ❧

Act Four Considerations

ACT FOUR Scene 1

▶ This scene marks the third time that Paris appears in the play and the first time that he meets with Juliet directly. What do you think of Shakespeare's characterization of Paris? To what extent is he a sympathetic or unsympathetic character? Why has Shakespeare portrayed him in this way?

▶ Juliet is perhaps guilty of gross exaggeration when she describes the six desperate things she is prepared to do rather than marry Paris. Modernize this list. Be creative and exaggerate.

▶ What is the Friar's plan? What has occurred or been said previously in this play to foreshadow the formulation of this strategy? Can you think of a better plan? In formulating your plan, keep in mind the restrictions that would have been in place four hundred years ago. What would work today would not necessarily be possible in the past.

ACT FOUR Scene 2

▶ What is the mood of this scene? How is the mood created?

▶ Write a cryptic horoscope for Capulet that deals with the events in this scene.

ACT FOUR Scene 3

▶ Shakespeare is considered a master at creating realistic characters. In this brief scene, Juliet displays a number of different traits that serve to illustrate the complexity and completeness of her character. What different aspects of her personality are portrayed in this scene?

ACT FOUR Scene 4

▶ What dramatic purpose is served by this scene?

ACT FOUR Scene 5

▶ In what ways does the mood change from the beginning to the end of this scene? Draw a diagram in which you trace the changes. What conclusions can you draw about Shakespeare's intentions from this diagram?

▶ Shakespeare does not provide us with a scene dramatizing Juliet's funeral. It is common at funerals for people who know the deceased to deliver eulogies. Write at least two short eulogies for Juliet. They can be written from the point of view of any of the following characters: Capulet, Lady Capulet, the Nurse, Paris, or Friar Laurence.

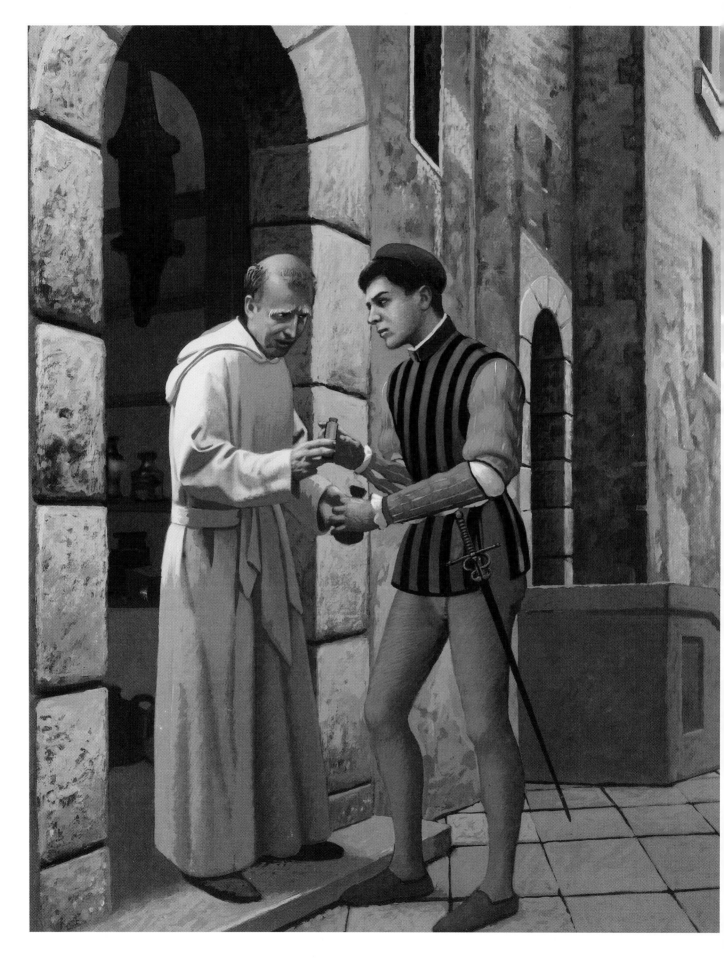

Act Five
Scene 1

Mantua. A street.

Balthasar travels to Mantua to inform Romeo that Juliet is dead and has been placed in the Capulet monument. Romeo is determined to join her in death and prepares to return to Verona that evening. He convinces a poor apothecary to sell him poison. It is now Thursday morning.

Enter Romeo.

ROMEO: If I may trust the flattering truth of sleep
My dreams presage some joyful news at hand.
My bosom's lord sits lightly in his throne,
And all this day an unaccustomed spirit
Lifts me above the ground with cheerful thoughts.
I dreamt my lady came and found me dead —
Strange dream that gives a dead man leave to think! —
And breathed such life with kisses in my lips
That I revived and was an emperor.
Ah me, how sweet is love itself possessed   10
When but love's shadows are so rich in joy.

Enter Romeo's man Balthasar.

News from Verona! How now, Balthasar?
Dost thou not bring me letters from the Friar?
How doth my lady? Is my father well?
How doth my Juliet? That I ask again,
For nothing can be ill if she be well.
BALTHASAR: Then she is well and nothing can be ill.
Her body sleeps in Capels' monument,
And her immortal part with angels lives.
I saw her laid low in her kindred's vault   20
And presently took post to tell it you.
O, pardon me for bringing these ill news,
Since you did leave it for my office, sir.
ROMEO: Is it even so? Then I defy you, stars!
Thou knowest my lodging. Get me ink and paper
And hire posthorses. I will hence tonight.

1. *flattering ... sleep –* dreams that give hope of good things to come
2. *presage –* foretell
3. *bosom's lord –* heart; love
4. *unaccustomed spirit –* unfamiliar sense of cheerfulness

11. *love's shadows –* dreams of love

17. *well –* The Elizabethans used an expression that suggested that "the dead are well" at rest. The word *well,* therefore, had a double meaning, and in this context Balthasar would not be lying.

21. *took post –* rode quickly (using post horses)

28. *import* – suggest

39. *apothecary* – one who mixes and sells drugs for medicine
41. *weeds* – clothes
41. *overwhelming* – overhanging
42. *Culling of simples* – gathering herbs for medicines
47. *beggarly account* – very small number
49. *packthread* – rope or twine
49. *cakes of roses* – cakes of compressed rose petals used for perfume
51. *penury* – poverty
53. *present* – immediate
54. *caitiff* – miserable

The role of Romeo "is badly placed in the play. The 'Banishment' scene ... becomes doubly difficult following as it does right on the heels of Juliet's great lamentation scene with the Nurse; and the Apothecary scene ... follows immediately on the long scene of wailing and grief over the supposed dead body of Juliet, which robs it of much of its effect."
– Sir John Gielgud (b. 1904), English Shakespearean actor

BALTHASAR: I do beseech you, sir, have patience.
    Your looks are pale and wild and do import
    Some misadventure.
ROMEO: Tush, thou art deceived.   30
    Leave me and do the thing I bid thee do.
    Hast thou no letters to me from the Friar?
BALTHASAR: No, my good lord.
ROMEO: No matter. Get thee gone
    And hire those horses. I'll be with thee straight.

Exit Balthasar.

Well, Juliet, I will lie with thee tonight.
Let's see for means. O mischief, thou art swift
To enter in the thoughts of desperate men.
I do remember an apothecary —
And hereabouts he dwells — which late I noted   40
In tattered weeds, with overwhelming brows,
Culling of simples. Meagre were his looks,
Sharp misery had worn him to the bones,
And in his needy shop a tortoise hung,
An alligator stuffed, and other skins
Of ill-shaped fishes; and about his shelves
A beggarly account of empty boxes,
Green earthen pots, bladders, and musty seeds,
Remnants of packthread, and old cakes of roses
Were thinly scattered to make up a show.   50
Noting this penury, to myself I said,
"And if a man did need a poison now
Whose sale is present death in Mantua,
Here lives a caitiff wretch would sell it him."
O, this same thought did but forerun my need,
And this same needy man must sell it me.
As I remember, this should be the house.
Being holiday, the beggar's shop is shut.
What, ho! apothecary!

Enter Apothecary.

APOTHECARY: Who calls so loud?   60
ROMEO: Come hither, man. I see that thou art poor.
    Hold, there is forty ducats. Let me have
    A dram of poison, such soon-speeding gear
    As will disperse itself through all the veins
    That the life-weary taker may fall dead,

And that the trunk may be discharged of breath
As violently as hasty powder fired
Doth hurry from the fatal cannon's womb.

APOTHECARY: Such mortal drugs I have, but Mantua's law
Is death to any he that utters them.   70

ROMEO: Art thou so bare and full of wretchedness
And fearest to die? Famine is in thy cheeks,
Need and oppression starveth in thy eyes,
Contempt and beggary hangs upon thy back.
The world is not thy friend, nor the world's law.
The world affords no law to make thee rich;
Then be not poor, but break it, and take this.

APOTHECARY: My poverty but not my will consents.

ROMEO: I pay thy poverty and not thy will.

APOTHECARY: Put this in any liquid thing you will   80
And drink it off, and if you had the strength
Of twenty men, it would dispatch you straight.

ROMEO: There is thy gold — worse poison to men's souls,
Doing more murder in this loathsome world
Than these poor compounds that thou mayst not sell.
I sell thee poison, thou hast sold me none.
Farewell, buy food and get thyself in flesh.
Come, cordial, and not poison, go with me
To Juliet's grave, for there must I use thee.

Exeunt.

70. *utters* – dispenses

88. *cordial* – a reviving drink;
heart medicine

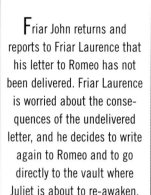

Friar John returns and reports to Friar Laurence that his letter to Romeo has not been delivered. Friar Laurence is worried about the consequences of the undelivered letter, and he decides to write again to Romeo and to go directly to the vault where Juliet is about to re-awaken.

Act Five
Scene 2

Verona. Friar Laurence's cell.

Enter Friar John.

FRIAR JOHN: Holy Franciscan Friar, Brother, ho!

Enter Friar Laurence.

F. LAURENCE: This same should be the voice of Friar John.
　　Welcome from Mantua. What says Romeo?
　　Or, if his mind be writ, give me his letter.
FRIAR JOHN: Going to find a barefoot brother out,
　　One of our order, to associate me
　　Here in this city visiting the sick,
　　And finding him, the searchers of the town,
　　Suspecting that we both were in a house
　　Where the infectious pestilence did reign,　　　　　10
　　Sealed up the doors, and would not let us forth,
　　So that my speed to Mantua there was stayed.
F. LAURENCE: Who bare my letter, then, to Romeo?
FRIAR JOHN: I could not send it — here it is again —
　　Nor get a messenger to bring it thee,
　　So fearful were they of infection.
F. LAURENCE: Unhappy fortune! By my brotherhood,
　　The letter was not nice, but full of charge,
　　Of dear import, and the neglecting it
　　May do much danger. Friar John, go hence,　　　　20
　　Get me an iron crow and bring it straight
　　Unto my cell.
FRIAR JOHN: Brother, I'll go and bring it thee.

Exit.

4. *mind* – message
5. *barefoot brother* – Franciscan
6. *associate* – accompany

8. *searchers* – During times of plague, *searchers* would view dead bodies to determine the cause of death. If they felt the cause was plague, they could quarantine the house.

12. *stayed* – prevented
18. *nice* – unimportant

21. *iron crow* – crowbar

F. Laurence: Now, must I to the monument alone.
Within this three hours will fair Juliet wake.
She will beshrew me much that Romeo
Hath had no notice of these accidents,
But I will write again to Mantua,
And keep her at my cell till Romeo come —
Poor living corse, closed in a dead man's tomb.   30

Exit.

26. *beshrew* – blame
27. *accidents* – events

"Strictly speaking —
and certainly if we take
Shakespeare's other
tragedies as a criterion —
we cannot admit *Romeo
and Juliet* as a tragedy at
all, for the catastrophe
depends on chance, the
undelivered letter of Friar
Lawrence. Without this
accident, all might have
been well."
– E.C. Pettet (b. 1949),
critic

Act Five
Scene 3

Verona.

A churchyard; in it the monument of the Capulets.

Enter Paris and his Page.

PARIS: Give me thy torch, boy. Hence, and stand aloof.
Yet put it out, for I would not be seen.
Under yond yew tree lay thee all along,
Holding thy ear close to the hollow ground.
So shall no foot upon the churchyard tread,
Being loose, unfirm, with digging up of graves,
But thou shalt hear it. Whistle then to me,
As signal that thou hearest something approach.
Give me those flowers. Do as I bid thee, go.

PAGE: I am almost afraid to stand alone   10
Here in the churchyard. Yet I will adventure.

[The Page retires.] Paris strews the tomb with flowers.

PARIS: Sweet flower, with flowers thy bridal bed I strew.
O woe, thy canopy is dust and stones
Which with sweet water nightly I will dew,
Or, wanting that, with tears distilled by moans.
The obsequies that I for thee will keep
Nightly shall be to strew, thy grave and weep.

Page whistles.

The boy gives warning something doth approach.
What cursed foot wanders this way tonight
To cross my obsequies and true love's rite?   20
What, with a torch? Muffle me, night, awhile.

It is late Thursday. Paris, who has come to Juliet's tomb to grieve and to strew flowers, encounters Romeo. They fight and Paris is killed. Romeo enters the monument, drinks the poison, and dies at Juliet's side. The Friar arrives just as Juliet re-awakens. When Juliet discovers that Romeo is dead, she in turn stabs herself. The Watch arrive and are soon followed by the Prince, the Capulets, and Montague. Friar Laurence and Balthasar are questioned and in the process the entire story of Romeo and Juliet's marriage and deaths is told.

1. *aloof* – distant
3. *all along* – stretched out flat on the ground

11. *adventure* – risk it

16. *obsequies* – funeral rites

20. *cross* – interrupt

[Paris retires.] Enter Romeo and Balthasar with a torch,
a mattock, and a crow of iron.

ROMEO: Give me that mattock and the wrenching iron.
Hold, take this letter. Early in the morning
See thou deliver it to my lord and father.
Give me the light. Upon thy life I charge thee,
Whatever thou hearest or seest, stand all aloof
And do not interrupt me in my course.
Why I descend into this bed of death
Is partly to behold my lady's face
But chiefly to take thence from her dead finger   30
A precious ring, a ring that I must use
In dear employment. Therefore hence, be gone.
But if thou, jealous dost return to pry
In what I farther shall intend to do,
By heaven, I will tear thee joint by joint
And strew this hungry churchyard with thy limbs.
The time and my intents are savage-wild,
More fierce and more inexorable far
Than empty tigers or the roaring sea.
BALTHASAR: I will be gone, sir, and not trouble you.   40
ROMEO: So shalt thou show me friendship. Take thou that.
Live, and be prosperous, and farewell, good fellow.
BALTHASAR: For all this same, I'll hide me hereabout.
His looks I fear, and his intents I doubt.

[Balthasar retires.]

ROMEO: Thou detestable maw, thou womb of death
Gorged with the dearest morsel of the earth,
Thus I enforce thy rotten jaws to open,
And in despite I'll cram thee with more food.

Romeo opens the tomb.

PARIS: This is that banished haughty Montague
That murdered my love's cousin — with which grief   50
It is supposed the fair creature died —
And here is come to do some villainous shame
To the dead bodies. I will apprehend him.
Stop thy unhallowed toil, vile Montague!
Can vengeance be pursued further than death?
Condemned villain, I do apprehend thee.
Obey, and go with me, for thou must die.

Stage Direction: *mattock* –
broad-edged pickaxe

mattock

33. *jealous* – curious

37. *time* – night
38. *inexorable far* –
determined
39. *empty* – ravenous,
hungry

45. *maw* – stomach (of a
monster). Romeo is referring
to the tomb.

53. *apprehend* – arrest

121

ROMEO: I must indeed, and therefore came I hither.
　　　　Good gentle youth, tempt not a desperate man.
　　　　Fly hence and leave me. Think upon these gone.　　60
　　　　Let them affright thee. I beseech thee, youth,
　　　　Put not another sin upon my head
　　　　By urging me to fury. O, be gone.
　　　　By heaven, I love thee better than myself,
　　　　For I come hither armed against myself.
　　　　Stay not, be gone, live, and hereafter say
　　　　A madman's mercy bid thee run away.

PARIS: I do defy thy conjuration
　　　　And apprehend thee for a felon here.

ROMEO: Wilt thou provoke me? Then have at thee, boy!　　70

They fight.

PAGE: O Lord, they fight! I will go call the watch.

[Page exits. Paris falls.]

PARIS: O, I am slain! If thou be merciful,
　　　　Open the tomb, lay me with Juliet.

[Paris dies.]

ROMEO: In faith, I will. Let me peruse this face.
　　　　Mercutio's kinsman, noble County Paris!
　　　　What said my man when my betossed soul
　　　　Did not attend him as we rode? I think
　　　　He told me Paris should have married Juliet.
　　　　Said he not so? Or did I dream it so?
　　　　Or am I mad, hearing him talk of Juliet　　　　80
　　　　To think it was so? O, give me thy hand,
　　　　One writ with me in sour misfortune's book!
　　　　I'll bury thee in a triumphant grave.
　　　　A grave? O, no, a lantern, slaughtered youth,
　　　　For here lies Juliet, and her beauty makes
　　　　This vault a feasting presence, full of light.
　　　　Death, lie thou there, by a dead man interred.
　　　　How oft when men are at the point of death
　　　　Have they been merry! Which their keepers call
　　　　A lightning before death. O, how may I　　　　90
　　　　Call this a lightning? O my love, my wife,
　　　　Death, that hath sucked the honey of thy breath,
　　　　Hath had no power yet upon thy beauty.

68. *conjuration* – appeals

76. *betossed* – disturbed
77. *attend* – listen
84. *lantern* – turret with many windows. Romeo thinks of the tomb as a brightly lit turret because Juliet's beauty fills the room with light.

lantern

90. *lightning* – revival of spirits

Thou art not conquered. Beauty's ensign yet
Is crimson in thy lips and in thy cheeks,
And death's pale flag is not advanced there.
Tybalt, liest thou there in thy bloody sheet?
O, what more favour can I do to thee
Than with that hand that cut thy youth in twain
To sunder his that was thine enemy?   100
Forgive me, cousin. Ah, dear Juliet,
Why art thou yet so fair? Shall I believe
That unsubstantial Death is amorous,
And that the lean abhorred monster keeps
Thee here in dark to be his paramour?
For fear of that I still will stay with thee
And never from this palace of dim night
Depart again. Here, here will I remain
With worms that are thy chambermaids. O, here
Will I set up my everlasting rest   110
And shake the yoke of inauspicious stars
From this world-wearied flesh. Eyes, look your last!
Arms, take your last embrace! And, lips, O you
The doors of breath, seal with a righteous kiss
A dateless bargain to engrossing Death!
Come, bitter conduct, come unsavoury guide,
Thou desperate pilot, now at once run on
The dashing rocks thy seasick weary bark.
Here's to my love!

                      [Drinks.]

                      O true apothecary!   120
Thy drugs are quick. Thus with a kiss I die.

          [Romeo] falls. Enter Friar [Laurence] with lantern, crow,
                              and spade.

FRIAR: Saint Francis be my speed! How oft tonight
          Have my old feet stumbled at graves! Who's there?
BALTHASAR: Here's one, a friend, and one that knows you well.
FRIAR: Bliss be upon you! Tell me, good my friend,
          What torch is yond that vainly lends his light
          To grubs and eyeless skulls? As I discern,
          It burneth in the Capels' monument.
BALTHASAR: It doth so, holy sir, and there's my master,
          One that you love.   130
FRIAR: Who is it?

"Character is destiny. Romeo is precipitate; he goes to the Capulet ball uninvited; he jumps over the garden wall to speak with the girl he has just met, he marries Juliet off-hand, he comes between Tybalt and Mercutio, he slays the bloody Tybalt and later slays himself at the tomb of his lover — it is all of a piece. The tragedy comes from the qualities of Romeo's character and not from an unfavorable star or frowning Providence."
– J.B. Henneman (1911), American professor

105. *paramour* – mistress

111. *inauspicious stars* – unfavourable stars

RELATED READING

Soft—Soft—She Breathes – drama by David Garrick (page 153)

116. *bitter conduct* – the poison that will serve as his guide to the afterlife

122. *Saint Francis* – of Assisi, who in 1210 founded the Franciscan order of monks

Act Five • Scene 3

BALTHASAR: Romeo.
FRIAR: How long hath he been there?
BALTHASAR: Full half an hour.
FRIAR: Go with me to the vault.
BALTHASAR: I dare not, sir.
    My master knows not but I am gone hence,
    And fearfully did menace me with death
    If I did stay to look on his intents.
FRIAR: Stay then, I'll go alone. Fear comes upon me.   140
    O, much I fear some ill unthrifty thing.
BALTHASAR: As I did sleep under this yew tree here
    I dreamt my master and another fought,
    And that my master slew him.
FRIAR: Romeo!

Friar stoops and looks on the blood and weapons.

Alack, alack, what blood is this which stains
The stony entrance of this sepulchre?
What mean these masterless and gory swords
To lie discoloured by this place of peace?

[Enters the tomb.]

Romeo! O, pale! Who else? What, Paris too?   150

141. *unthrifty* – unfortunate

147. *sepulchre* – tomb

And steeped in blood? Ah, what an unkind hour
Is guilty of this lamentable chance!
The lady stirs.

Juliet rises.

JULIET: O comfortable Friar, where is my lord?
    I do remember well where I should be,
    And there I am. Where is my Romeo?
FRIAR: I hear some noise. Lady, come from that nest
    Of death, contagion, and unnatural sleep.
    A greater power than we can contradict
    Hath thwarted our intents. Come, come away.   160
    Thy husband in thy bosom there lies dead,
    And Paris too. Come, I'll dispose of thee
    Among a sisterhood of holy nuns.
    Stay not to question, for the Watch is coming.
    Come, go, good Juliet. I dare no longer stay.
JULIET: Go, get thee hence, for I will not away.

Exit Friar Laurence.

What's here? A cup, closed in my true love's hand?
Poison, I see, hath been his timeless end.
O churl. Drunk all, and left no friendly drop

154. *comfortable* – comfort-giving

"The age of Juliet seems to be the key to her character throughout the play, an essential ingredient in the intense sympathy which she inspires; ... interest is heightened and redoubled when ... you add all the kind affectations with which you share in the joys and sorrows of the child. There is childishness in the discourse of Juliet, and the poet has shown us why; because she scarcely ceased to be a child." John Quincy Adams (1767 – 1848), sixth president of the United States

169. *churl* – inconsiderate one; miser

172. *restorative* – Romeo's kiss, despite the poison, would be like a restorative to Juliet.

> Though lovers be lost, love shall not
> and death shall have no dominion
> – Dylan Thomas (1914 – 1953), Welsh poet and playwright

179. *attach* – arrest

186. *ground* – playing with double meaning of "ground" – earth and cause

187. *circumstance descry* – more information discover

To help me after? I will kiss thy lips.   170
Haply some poison yet doth hang on them
To make me die with a restorative.

[Kisses him.]

Thy lips are warm!
1 WATCHMAN: *[Within.]* Lead, boy. Which way?
JULIET: Yea, noise? Then I'll be brief. O happy dagger.
　　This is thy sheath. There rust, and let me die.

She stabs herself and falls.
Enter [Paris's] Page and Watchmen.

PAGE: This is the place. There, where the torch doth burn.
1 WATCHMAN: The ground is bloody. Search about the
　　churchyard.
　　Go, some of you. Whoever you find, attach.

[Exeunt some of the Watch.]

Pitiful sight! Here lies the County slain   180
And Juliet bleeding, warm, and newly dead,
Who here hath lain this two days buried.
Go, tell the Prince. Run to the Capulets.
Raise up the Montagues. Some others search.

[Exeunt others of the Watch.]

We see the ground whereon these woes do lie,
But the true ground of all these piteous woes
We cannot without circumstance descry.

Enter [some of the Watch, with] Balthasar.

2 WATCHMAN: Here's Romeo's man. We found him in the
　　churchyard.
1 WATCHMAN: Hold him in safety till the Prince come hither.

Enter Friar Laurence and another Watchman.

3 WATCHMAN: Here is a friar that trembles, sighs, and
　　weeps.   190
　　We took this mattock and this spade from him
　　As he was coming from this churchyard side.
1 WATCHMAN: A great suspicion! Stay the friar too.

Enter the Prince [and Attendants].

PRINCE: What misadventure is so early up,
That calls our person from our morning rest?

Enter Capulet and Lady Capulet [and Servants].

CAPULET: What should it be, that is so shrieked abroad?
LADY CAPULET: O, the people in the street cry "Romeo,"
Some "Juliet," and some "Paris," and all run,
With open outcry, toward our monument.
PRINCE: What fear is this which startles in our ears?   200
1 WATCHMAN: Sovereign, here lies the County Paris slain,
And Romeo dead, and Juliet, dead before,
Warm and new killed.
PRINCE: Search, seek, and know how this foul murder comes.
1 WATCHMAN: Here is a friar, and slaughtered Romeo's man,
With instruments upon them fit to open
These dead men's tombs.
CAPULET: O heavens! O wife, look how our daughter bleeds!
This dagger hath mistaken, for, lo, his house
Is empty on the back of Montague,   210
And it mis-sheathed in my daughter's bosom!
LADY CAPULET: O me! This sight of death is as a bell
That warns my old age to a sepulchre.

Enter Montague [and Servants].

PRINCE: Come, Montague, for thou art early up
To see thy son and heir now early down.
MONTAGUE: Alas, my liege, my wife is dead tonight.
Grief of my son's exile hath stopped her breath.
What further woe conspires against mine age?
PRINCE: Look, and thou shalt see.
MONTAGUE: O thou untaught! What manners is in this,   220
To press before thy father to a grave?
PRINCE: Seal up the mouth of outrage for a while,
Till we can clear these ambiguities
And know their spring, their head, their true descent;
And then will I be general of your woes
And lead you, even to death. Meantime forbear,
And let mischance be slave to patience.
Bring forth the parties of suspicion.
FRIAR: I am the greatest, able to do least,
Yet most suspected, as the time and place   230
Doth make against me, of this direful murder.
And here I stand, both to impeach and purge
Myself condemned and myself excused.

"Tragedy would not be a tragedy if it were not a painful mystery."
– A.C. Bradley
(1851 – 1935), British scholar and critic

209. *house* – sheath

220 – 221. The complaint here is that young Romeo should have learned about death by having to deal with his father's death. Romeo is accused of being without manners for not waiting his turn and for rushing ahead to his grave before his father.

222. *outrage* – outcry, loud grief
225. *general* – leader
227. "And bear your suffering with patience."
232 – 233. *impeach ... excused* – accuse myself of those things for which I should be condemned and excuse myself of those charges of which I am innocent

235. *I will be brief* – Can the Friar be brief? The Friar has the two longest speeches in the play. This is the second longest. (In the play *Hamlet,* Polonius states that "Brevity is the soul of wit," and then proceeds at length to illustrate that he has no wit because he cannot be brief.) However, at this point in the play, we need someone like the Friar to tie up all the loose ends for the survivors. The Elizabethans did not like endings that were not fully resolved. The Friar fulfills this function fully.

249. *art* – skill (in medicines)
257. *stayed* – delayed, prevented

"Rancour has been converted to love. That which is base has been transmuted into gold. Juliet and her Romeo, who at the outset of the play claims to have 'a soul of lead' (1.4.15), are now converted to statues of pure gold."
– Lyndy Abraham, professor, University of New South Wales

272. *privy* – in on the secret
272. *aught* – anything

275. *rigour* – severity

PRINCE: Then say it once what thou dost know in this.
FRIAR: I will be brief, for my short date of breath
    Is not so long as is a tedious tale.
    Romeo, there dead, was husband to that Juliet,
    And she, there dead, that Romeo's faithful wife.
    I married them, and their stolen marriage day
    Was Tybalt's doomsday, whose untimely death   240
    Banished the new-made bridegroom from this city;
    For whom, and not for Tybalt, Juliet pined.
    You, to remove that siege of grief from her,
    Betrothed and would have married her perforce
    To County Paris. Then comes she to me
    And with wild looks bid me devise some mean
    To rid her from this second marriage,
    Or in my cell there would she kill herself.
    Then gave I her — so tutored by my art —
    A sleeping potion, which so took effect   250
    As I intended, for it wrought on her
    The form of death. Meantime I writ to Romeo
    That he should hither come as this dire night
    To help to take her from her borrowed grave,
    Being the time the potion's force should cease.
    But he which bore my letter, Friar John,
    Was stayed by accident, and yesternight
    Returned my letter back. Then all alone
    At the prefixed hour of her waking
    Came I to take her from her kindred's vault,   260
    Meaning to keep her closely at my cell
    Till I conveniently could send to Romeo.
    But when I came, some minute ere the time
    Of her awaking, here untimely lay
    The noble Paris and true Romeo dead.
    She wakes, and I entreated her come forth
    And bear this work of heaven with patience,
    But then a noise did scare me from the tomb,
    And she, too desperate, would not go with me,
    But, as it seems, did violence on herself.   270
    All this I know, and to the marriage
    Her Nurse is privy. And if aught in this
    Miscarried by my fault, let my old life
    Be sacrificed, some hour before his time,
    Unto the rigour of severest law.
PRINCE: We still have known thee for a holy man.
    Where's Romeo's man? What can he say to this?
BALTHASAR: I brought my master news of Juliet's death,

And then in post he came from Mantua
To this same place, to this same monument. 280
This letter he early bid me give his father,
And threatened me with death, going in the vault,
If I departed not and left him there.
PRINCE: Give me the letter. I will look on it.
Where is the County's Page that raised the Watch?
Sirrah, what made your master in this place?
PAGE: He came with flowers to strew his lady's grave,
And bid me stand aloof, and so I did.
Anon comes one with light to ope the tomb
And by and by my master drew on him, 290
And then I ran away to call the Watch.
PRINCE: This letter doth make good the Friar's words,
Their course of love, the tidings of her death,
And here he writes that he did buy a poison
Of a poor pothecary, and therewithal
Came to this vault to die, and lie with Juliet.
Where be these enemies? Capulet, Montague,
See what a scourge is laid upon your hate,
That heaven finds means to kill your joys with love!
And I, for winking at your discords too, 300
Have lost a brace of kinsmen. All are punished.
CAPULET: O brother Montague, give me thy hand.
This is my daughter's jointure, for no more
Can I demand.
MONTAGUE: But I can give thee more;
For I will raise her statue in pure gold,
That whiles Verona by that name is known,
There shall no figure at such rate be set
As that of true and faithful Juliet.
CAPULET: As rich shall Romeo's by his lady's lie, 310
Poor sacrifices of our enmity!
PRINCE: A glooming peace this morning with it brings.
The sun for sorrow will not show his head.
Go hence, to have more talk of these sad things.
Some shall be pardoned, and some punished,
For never was a story of more woe
Than this of Juliet and her Romeo.

Exeunt omnes.

FINIS.

"The last line of the play, which reverses the order of the appearance of the heroes in the title — 'For never was a story of more woe/Than this of Juliet and her Romeo' — making Romeo the one who belongs to Juliet rather than the other way around, cannot only express the necessities of rhyme."
– Francois Laroque

300. *winking* – closing my eyes; tolerating
301. *brace* – pair. The Prince has now lost two kinsmen – Mercutio and Paris.
303. *jointure* – gift from the groom's family to the bride. A handshake in friendship is all that Capulet desires.

315. *Some shall be pardoned, and some punished* – Shakespeare does not elaborate on this. In Arthur Brooke's poem *Romeus and Juliet,* we learn that the Nurse was banished because she hid the marriage from Juliet's parents, that Romeo's servant went unpunished because all he did was obey his master, that the apothecary was hanged for breaking the law by selling poison, and Friar Laurence was found to be without fault because of his lifelong good service to the community. Of his own accord, Friar Laurence exiled himself to a hermitage, where he died five years later.

Act Five Considerations

ACT FIVE Scene 1

▶ Describe Romeo's dream. Review the first four acts of the play, taking note of the other references to dreams and premonitions. What conclusions can you draw from Shakespeare's use of dreams and premonitions in this play?

▶ In two out of the three different editions of the play published during the Elizabethan period, Romeo reacts to Balthasar's news by saying: "Then I *deny* you, stars!" This edition follows the third version: "Then I *defy* you, stars!" What different ideas do these two variations convey? Which do you prefer?

▶ What does this scene reveal about the changes that have occurred in Romeo's character?

▶ Why does Shakespeare have Romeo go on at length describing the appearance of the Apothecary's shop?

ACT FIVE Scene 2

▶ Imagine that you are Friar Laurence. Write the letter that Friar John was asked to deliver to Romeo. Then write the second letter that Friar Laurence intends to write to Romeo.

▶ Friar Laurence's first letter is not delivered due to chance and circumstance. Some scholars argue that because Shakespeare relied too heavily on chance or coincidence, this play is not a true tragedy. What other examples of chance or coincidence are there in this play?

ACT FIVE Scene 3

▶ In the first 21 lines of this scene, Shakespeare portrays Paris in such a way that the audience cannot help but be reminded of Romeo in the first scene of the play. What similarities do you see between the early Romeo and Paris as he is characterized in this scene?

▶ Some film versions of the play omit the Paris sequence. What are the advantages and disadvantages of deleting this part of the play? What purpose, in other words, is served by having Romeo and Paris fight?

▶ Shakespeare could easily have ended this story differently. Write your own ending to this play. Be sure that you resolve all the loose ends in the plot.

The 10 Most Challenging Questions about *Romeo and Juliet*

Shakespeare's works have survived for over 400 years. His plays continue to be read, studied, performed, and enjoyed by people all over the world. Shakespeare's legacy consists of a host of unforgettable characters involved in great stories, speaking classic lines that contain some of the most powerful poetry ever written.

Perhaps another important reason why Shakespeare continues to fascinate readers and audiences is that his plays can be interpreted in so many different ways. It is indeed ironic that Shakespeare's most frustrating quality could well be his greatest strength.

The play *Romeo and Juliet* poses a number of very interesting and challenging questions. You are invited to choose one or more of the following for closer focus and study. The end result of your efforts may take the form of a research essay, an independent study project, or a position paper. To address these questions, you will need to probe the text carefully and consult secondary sources. You must also be prepared to take a stand regarding the issues.

1. How bitter is the "ancient grudge" between the Montagues and the Capulets? Putting aside the street brawl early in the first scene of the play, what evidence is there that the animosity between the two families is as strong as ever or has subsided?

2. What valid dramatic purposes do the prologues serve in this play? What does Shakespeare have Benvolio say about prologues at the beginning of Act One, Scene 4? Using CD-ROM or Internet search tools, find what Shakespeare has to say about prologues in some of his other plays. How do you feel about the prologues in this play? Justify or criticize their inclusion in this tragedy by discussing the purposes served and effects created through their use.

3. Who is the protagonist of the story, Romeo or Juliet? Consider who acts more maturely and who undergoes the most character development. Consider also why Shakespeare never shows us any scenes involving the Montague household.

4. The play poses a number of questions that have puzzled readers for centuries. For example: a) Why does Paris not appear at the Capulet party? b) In Act Three, Scene 1, why does Benvolio disappear without mention after reporting the details of the deaths of Mercutio and Tybalt? c) How old is Lady Capulet? In Act Five, Scene 3, she refers to her old age; but in Act One, Scene 3, she claims she was a mother by the time she was Juliet's age.

   Choose one of the above questions, and research what others have said about the issue. Indicate the various answers to the question, and then defend your position on the matter.

5. Is *Romeo and Juliet* a true story? Were the two title characters based on real people? Research the sources of the play. Summarize the basic plots of these sources and discuss Shakespeare's treatment of these sources.

6. Of all the minor characters in the play, who was the most responsible for contributing to the deaths of Romeo and Juliet? Was it the Nurse, Friar Laurence, Capulet, Tybalt, Mercutio, or the Apothecary?

7. Why do Romeo and Juliet kill themselves at the end of the play?

8. Is *Romeo and Juliet* a sophisticated "morality play"? What are morality plays? How did they develop and what debt does Shakespeare owe to this form of literature? Based on what you have learned about morality plays, what do you think would be the moral lessons that the Elizabethan audience would get from *Romeo and Juliet*?

9. Who is the villain in this play? Most tragedies have a villain. Is *Romeo and Juliet* an exception? To what extent can one consider Tybalt to be the villain? Is there anyone else who could fit the role of villain in this play?

10. Are Romeo and Juliet true tragic heroes or victims of fate? To answer this question you will need to research the characteristics of classical tragedy and the tragic hero, and determine the extent to which the play conforms to the conventions of classical tragedy. You will also need to decide what role fate and the feud play in the tragedy.

The ARGUMENT from ROMEUS and JULIET

Shakespeare based his play on Arthur Brooke's long poem Romeus and Juliet. *Here is the argument, or prologue, to that work.*

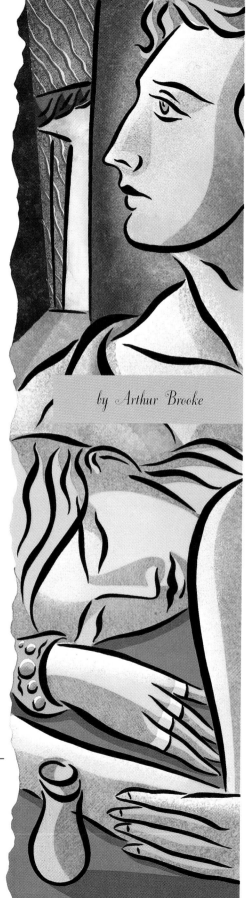

by Arthur Brooke

Love hath inflamed twain by sudden sight,
And both do grant the thing that both desire:
They wed in shrift, by counsel of a friar.
Young Romeus climbs fair Juliet's bower by night,
Three months he doth enjoy his chief delight.
By Tybalt's rage, provoked unto ire,
He payeth death to Tybalt for his hire.
A banished man, he 'scapes by secret flight,
New marriage is offered to his wife.
She drinks a drink that seems to reave her breath:
They bury her, that sleeping yet hath life.
Her husband hears the tidings of her death:
He drinks his bane. And she with Romeus' knife,
When she awakes, her self, alas! she slayeth.

Compare Shakespeare's prologue to Brooke's. Which contains more information? Which do you prefer? Explain.

Assuming that an argument provides an introduction to the plot, characters, and theme of a work, what does this prologue suggest will be the focus of Brooke's work?

LIGHT IMAGES *in* ROMEO AND JULIET

by Caroline F. E. Spurgeon

According to this classic study of imagery, the play Romeo and Juliet *is dominated by the "glory of sunlight and starlight in a dark world."*

In *Romeo and Juliet* the beauty and ardour of young love are seen by Shakespeare as the irradiating glory of sunlight and starlight in a dark world. The dominating image is *light*, every form and manifestation of it: the sun, moon, stars, fire, lightning, the flash of gunpowder, and the reflected light of beauty and of love; while by contrast we have night, darkness, clouds, rain, mist, and smoke.

Each of the lovers thinks of the other as light; Romeo's overpowering impression when he first catches sight of Juliet on the fateful evening at the Capulets' ball is seen in his exclamation,

> *O, she doth teach the torches to burn bright!*
> *It seems she hangs upon the cheek of night*
> *Like a rich jewel in an Ethiop's ear.*

To Juliet, Romeo is "day in night"; to Romeo, Juliet is the sun rising from the east, and when they soar to love's ecstasy, each alike pictures the other as stars in heaven, shedding such brightness as puts to shame the heavenly bodies themselves. . . .

Thus Romeo plays with the old conceit that two of the fairest stars in heaven, having some business on earth, have entreated Juliet's eyes to take their place till they return, and he conjectures,

> *What if her eyes were there, they in her head?*

If so,

> *The brightness of her cheek would shame*
> *those stars,*

> *As daylight doth a lamp;*

and then comes the rush of feeling, the overpowering realisation and immortal expression of the transforming glory of love:

> *her eyes in heaven*
> *Would through the airy region stream so*
> *bright*
> *That birds would sing and think it were*
> *not night.*

And Juliet['s] . . . lover to her not only radiates light, but is, indeed, very light itself:

> *Give me my Romeo; and, when he shall die,*
> *Take him and cut him out in little stars,*
> *And he will make the face of heaven so fine,*
> *That all the world will be in love with night,*
> *And pay no worship to the garish sun.*

Love is described by Romeo, before he knows what it really is, as

> *a smoke raised with the fume of sighs;*
> *Being purged, a fire sparkling in lovers' eyes;*

and the messengers of love are pictured by Juliet, when she is chafing under the nurse's delay as . . . the swift, magical, transforming power of light:

> *love's heralds [she cries] should be*
> *thoughts,*
> *Which ten times faster glide than the*
> *sun's beams,*
> *Driving back shadows over louring hills.*

The irradiating quality of the beauty of love is noticed by both lovers; by Juliet, in her first ecstasy, when she declares that lovers' "own beauties" are sufficient light for them to see by, and, at the end, by Romeo, when, thinking her dead, he gazes on her and cries,

> *her beauty makes*
> *This vault a feasting presence full of light.*

There can be no question, I think, that Shakespeare saw the story, in its swift and tragic beauty, as an almost blinding flash of light, suddenly ignited, and as swiftly quenched. He quite deliberately compresses the action from over nine months to the almost incredibly short period of five days; so that the lovers meet on Sunday, are wedded on Monday, part at dawn on Tuesday and are reunited in death on the night of Thursday. The sensation of swiftness and brilliance, accompanied by danger and destruction, is accentuated again and again; by Juliet, when she avows their betrothal

> *is too rash, too unadvised, too sudden,*
> *Too like the lightning, which doth cease to be*
> *Ere one can say "It lightens";*

and by Romeo and the friar, who instinctively make repeated use of the image of the quick destructive flash of gunpowder. Indeed the friar, in his well-known answer to Romeo's prayer for instant marriage, succinctly, in the last nine words, sums up the whole movement of the play:

> *These violent delights have violent ends,*
> *And in their triumph die; like fire and powder*
> *Which as they kiss consume.*

Even old Capulet, whom one does not think of as a poetical person, though he uses many images—some of great beauty—carries on the idea of light to represent love and youth and beauty, and of the clouding of the sun for grief and sorrow. He promises Paris that on the evening of the ball he shall see at his house

> *Earth-treading stars that make dark*
> *heaven light;*

and when he encounters Juliet weeping, as he thinks, for her cousin Tybalt's death, he clothes his comment in similar nature imagery of light quenched in darkness:

> *When the sun sets, the air doth drizzle dew;*
> *But for the sunset of my brother's son*
> *It rains downright.*

In addition to this more definite symbolic imagery, we find that radiant light, sunshine, starlight, moonbeams, sunrise and sunset, the sparkle of fire, a meteor, candles, torches, quick-coming darkness, clouds, mist, rain and night, form a pictorial background, or running accompaniment, to the play. . . .

We meet it at once in the prince's description of the attitude of the rival houses

> *That quench the fire of your pernicious rage*
> *With purple fountains issuing from your*
> *veins;*

and later, in the talk of Benvolio and Montague about the rising sun, the dew and clouds, followed by Romeo's definition of love, Capulet's words just quoted, Benvolio's rhyming proverb about fire, the talk of Romeo and Mercutio about torches, candles, lights, and lamps, the flashing lights and torches of the ball, four times accentuated, Romeo's conception of Juliet as a "bright angel,"

> *As glorious to this night, . . .*
> *As is a winged messenger of heaven;*

in the moonlight in the orchard, the sunrise Friar Lawrence watches from his cell, the sun clearing from heaven Romeo's sighs, the exquisite light and shadow swiftly chasing over Juliet's words in the orchard, the "black fate" of the day on which Mercutio was killed, the "fire-eyed fury" which leads Romeo to challenge Tybalt, their fight, to which they go "like lightning," the sunset which Juliet so ardently desires to be swift "and bring in cloudy night immediately," the exquisite play of quivering light from darkness through dawn, till

jocund day
Stands tiptoe on the misty mountain tops,

which forms the theme of the lovers' parting song; and, at the last, in Romeo's anguished reply to Juliet, pointing out the contrast between the coming day and their own great sorrow:

More light and light: more dark and dark our woes!

And then, at the end, we see the darkness of the churchyard, lit by the glittering torch of Paris, quickly quenched; Romeo's arrival with his torch, the swift fight and death, the dark vault, which is not a grave but a lantern irradiated by Juliet's beauty, Romeo's grim jest on the "lightning before death," followed immediately by the self-slaughter of the "star-crossed" lovers, the gathering together of the stricken mourners as the day breaks, and the "glooming" peace of the overcast morning when

The sun for sorrow will not show his head.

Shakespeare's extraordinary susceptibility to suggestion and readiness to borrow are well exemplified in this running imagery. He took the idea from the last place we should expect, from the wooden doggerel of Arthur Brooke, and the germ of it is in the sing-song line in which Brooke describes the attitude of the lovers:

For each of them to other is as to the world the sun.

Their mutual feeling and the feud of the families are constantly referred to by Brooke as "fire" or "flame"; in the beginning, he speaks of the feud as a "mighty fire"; the families "bathe in blood of smarting

wounds," and the prince hopes he may "quench the sparks that burned within their breast." These three images are combined and unified by Shakespeare in the two lines already quoted:

That quench the fire of your pernicious rage
With purple fountains issuing from your veins

Other suggestions also come from Brooke, such as the emphasis on the bright light of the torches at the ball; Romeo's first sight of Juliet, which is a "sudden kindled fire"; her first impression of him, when he

in her sight did seem to pass the rest as far
As Phoebus' shining beams do pass the brightness of a star;

and his description in his first talk to her, of the

quick sparks and glowing furious glead
. . . from your beauty's pleasant eyne,
Love caused to proceed
Which have so set on fire each feeling part of mine
That lo, my mind doth melt away, my outward parts do pine,

which is transmuted by Shakespeare to the delightful image of the stars which have changed places with her eyes.

But although Shakespeare took the idea from [Brooke's] original, it scarcely needs saying that in taking it, he has transformed a few conventional and obvious similes of little poetic worth into a continuous and consistent running image of exquisite beauty, building up a definite picture and atmosphere of brilliance swiftly quenched, which powerfully affects the imagination of the reader. ■

Using magazine illustrations or original artwork, create a collage or poster that brings to life Spurgeon's conclusions about the imagery in *Romeo and Juliet.*

Another dominating series of images deals with ships and pilots. Find as many examples as you can of these images. What ideas does Shakespeare develop through this series of images?

Related Readings

based on a work
by Philarete Chasles

The romantic, dreamy atmosphere of Shakespeare's Verona is what appeals to many readers of Romeo and Juliet. *Shakespeare succeeds in creating a world that is at once enchanting and unforgettable.*

Who Cannot Recall

Who cannot recall lovely summer nights
when the forces of nature seem ripe for development
    and yet sunk in drowsy languor, —
intense heat mingled with exuberant vigor, fervid force,
    and silent freshness?

The nightingale's song comes from the depths of the grove.
The calices of the flowers are half-closed.
A pale lustre illumines the foliage of the forest,
    and the outline of the hills.

This profound repose conceals, we feel, a fertile force;
beneath the retiring melancholy of nature
    lies hidden burning emotions.
Beneath the pallor and coolness of night and its luminary
    there is a hint of restrained impetuosity —
    each flower, brooding in silence, is longing to bloom forth.

Such is the peculiar atmosphere
    with which Shakespeare has surrounded
    one of his most wonderful creations, *Romeo and Juliet.*

WHAT the MOON SAW

based on a work
by Hans Christian Andersen

Heavy clouds obscured the sky,
and the Moon did not make his appearance at all.
I stood in my little room,
more lonely than ever, and looked up at the sky
where he ought to have shown himself . . .

When Romeo climbed the balcony,
and the promise of true love fluttered
like a cherub toward heaven,
the round Moon hung,
half hidden among the dark cypresses,
in the lucid air . . .

Ah!
What tales the Moon can tell.
Human life is like a story to him . . .
And, as I looked dreamily towards the clouds,
the sky became bright.
There was a glancing light,
and a beam from the Moon fell upon me.
It vanished again,
and dark clouds flew past:
but still it was a greeting,
a friendly good-night
offered
        to me
           by the Moon.

Which poem do you think best succeeds in capturing the atmosphere of the play?

Write your own "What the Moon Saw" poem. Choose another incident in the play and describe it as the moon would have seen it.

Related Readings

by *Irving Shulman*

Excerpt from
WEST SIDE STORY

In the early 1960s, audiences all over the world were treated to a modernized version of the story of Romeo and Juliet. West Side Story first made its mark as a Broadway musical, then as a hit feature film, and finally as a novelization of the film—from which this excerpt is taken. The story takes place in the Upper West Side of New York City, and instead of feuding Capulets and Montagues, there are warring rival gangs, the Jets and the Sharks. The following excerpt describes the fateful first meeting of Maria and Tony at a local dance.

From the moment he had arrived at the dance, Tony had felt out of place. He hadn't brought a date and everyone there was paired off. And when he saw Bernardo and the Sharks, Riff and the Jets, they all seemed like foreigners. If he moved toward the door, no one would notice and he could get away. If Riff were stupid enough to challenge Bernardo, that was his business.

Then he saw the girl in the white dress standing against the wall. And as he saw her, she saw him, and any thought he had of leaving was gone. As if he were being led, Tony Wyzek approached Maria Nunez, looked into her dark eyes, stretched out his hands, and was led by her into another land.

The mambo had ended and a lighter, slower record had been placed on the turntable. As Tony drifted onto the dance floor, he gently clasped her fingers and looked down at her heart-shaped face, her liquid brown eyes, her lovely mouth just touched with lipstick. He nodded to approve of her dress which was white, beautiful, so different from anything worn by the other girls.

His fingers barely touched her back. Her touch on his shoulder was light, fragile; when he moved her through a turn and his hand pressed more firmly, she shuddered and moved as if to leave him, so Tony tightened his fingers only for a moment, then relaxed them.

There was nothing to fear, he told the girl. Never having been in this land before, he knew it well. It was a gentle land of green fields, warm winds, brilliant birds and perfumed flowers; no matter that they walked on clouds, they would not fall. Although he heard the music, it was as if from a distance.

Maria felt that her heart might burst. Were the lights above them dimmed so that she could not see this Anglo boy with whom she danced? And why wasn't she frightened of him? Why didn't he look, act, speak, as Bernardo said the Anglos did?

The night was hot, she felt perspiration trickle down the small of her back, but the fingers of this boy were so cool, and he danced so easily, without pressing against her, without trying to "sock it in," which was how Bernardo described Anglo dancing. But she had seen how Bernardo danced with Anita, how all the Sharks danced with their girls, so they were no different from the Jets.

"You're not thinking I'm someone else?" she heard him ask. It was a good voice, very shy.

Maria shook her head. "I know you're not."

"Or that we've met before?" Tony asked instead of shouting with joy that the girl wasn't going to leave him. He was certain of that now. This was as it had to be in this land: people who entered together remained there together, forever.

"I know we have not," Maria replied. "I . . . I'm glad I came to this dance."

"So am I. You know, I was just leaving. Then I saw you, and I got the message."

She was puzzled. "What message, please?"

Thinking was one thing, expressing it another. He wet his lips, then began slowly. "I don't know. Last couple of months I've been sort of going around asking myself: Who am I? What was I doing? Where was I going? Was something big ever going to happen to me? Sometimes I get so low my . . . excuse me," he stammered. "I mean, I'd feel so blue, wondering if I wasn't kidding myself about the thing that was gonna happen. Do you understand what I'm getting at?"

This was as it had to be in this land: people who entered together remained there together, forever.

"I think so." Maria was grave. What wonderful eyes this boy had. She had never heard it explained better by anyone. "Of course I understand," she added, hesitated, and decided to continue. "I felt that way on the airplane."

"I've never been in a plane," he said. "It must be wonderful."

Conscious that the music had ended, Tony was glad that they had danced toward a corner where there was a bench. "You know," he began, after they were seated, "you seem to know what I'm gonna say even before I say it." Her fingers rested on the edge of the bench, and he covered them with his hand. "They're cold," he said.

"Yours too." Gently she raised her free hand to touch his cheek, as she had done earlier that evening to Chino. The skin was rougher, no warmer, but her fingertips felt as if they had touched a live electric wire. "Your cheek is warm."

Tony dared to touch her chin. "You're warm too."

"But of course," Maria smiled. "They are the same. And it is warm. It is—"

"Humid?" He supplied the word and was pleased that she nodded.

"Yes," she thanked him. "But still it is not the warm of weather."

"You know what I just saw when you said that? Fireworks," he continued, after she nodded. "Great big pinwheels and rockets. But no sound, only lights. There—" his forefinger traced a trajectory "—see them?"

"Yes," she said. "They are beautiful."

"You're not kidding? Not saying it to make me feel foolish? You really see them?"

Maria traced a cross above her heart. "I

Related Readings

have not yet learned how to joke that way, and now . . ."

" . . . yes?"

"I think I never will."

The rockets were rising, joining together to explode in hearts and stars before they descended in a waterfall of light. Impulsively, because her hand was almost at his mouth, Tony moved his lips to kiss her palm. And as he did, he felt her tremble.

He leaned forward to smell the lovely sachet of her hair and the fragrance of light perfume, and to kiss her lips, so gently the boundaries of the magic land were not violated. Then he felt a rough hand on his shoulder that almost flung him from the bench.

Years of street fighting, of instant feline reflexes to sudden assault helped Tony bounce to his feet. His hands, formed into hard fists to throw at his target, were never launched, for he saw that Bernardo had turned away from him to look down at the girl on the bench.

He saw the destruction of their magic land. Of course, he had seen the girl come in with Bernardo. The girl in the white dress, whose name he did not even know, was Bernardo's sister. Tony was overwhelmed and terrified that he might lose the most wonderful thing he had ever found.

"Go home, American," Bernardo spat at him.

"Slow down, Bernardo," Tony said, and moved his right hand to assure the girl that everything was all right, that she could depend upon him not to fight.

Bernardo's lips twitched. "Stay away from my sister!" He turned to Maria. "Couldn't you see he was one of them?"

"No," she replied. "I saw only him, and he's done nothing wrong."

Snapping his fingers to gather the Sharks around him, Bernardo saw Chino moving rapidly across the dance floor. "I told you," he accused Maria, "there's only one thing they want from a Puerto Rican girl!"

"You're lying in your throat," Tony said.

"Cool, boy," Riff approved, as he got to Tony's side. "You tell him."

Chino tapped Bernardo's shoulder and moved past him to confront Tony. Very pale, but quiet, so that he did not look frightened, Chino measured the tall American. "Get away," he said. "Leave her alone."

"Keep out of this, Chino," Tony advised him, then turned away abruptly, fearful that Maria was going to leave.

Bernardo clamped his fingers around Maria's wrist to pull her behind him. "Now let me tell you . . . "

" . . . tell me!" Riff pushed forward. "If you characters want to settle this right here outside . . ."

Murray Benowitz knew that he was shouting, but he had to get their attention. "Fellows, please! Everything was going so well. Do you fellows get pleasure out of making trouble? Come on now, it won't hurt you to have a good time." With upward gestures of his right hand, he signaled frantically for the music to start again. "Everybody dance," he suggested. "Do it for me." ■

In groups of two or more, identify the similarities between the first meeting of Shakespeare's two lovers and Tony and Maria's first encounter. Do not just identify plot elements. Look also for parallels in characters and imagery.

The lovers in this story come from two different ethnic groups. If you were rewriting this story in a different setting, what two other groups could you use to create the effect of an "ancient grudge"? Write a short story similar to this excerpt in which two lovers from different backgrounds meet.

Related Readings

by Peggy Ashcroft

 On

Playing Juliet

Peggy Ashcroft is considered one of the greatest Shakespearean actors of the twentieth century. She has performed with all the great names in the theatre world and has taken on the role of Juliet several times. Here she recalls the unique challenges of playing Juliet.

Every Shakespearean actor is frequently asked to name a favourite play or part. There isn't really an answer, although I would unhesitatingly put both the title part and the play *Romeo and Juliet* in my top . . . four. There has been a recent fashion in the theatre to define a certain kind of play as a "black comedy." I would define *Romeo and Juliet* as a "golden tragedy." George Meredith wrote:

> *. . . In tragic life, God wot,*
> *No villain need be! Passions spin the plot:*
> *We are betrayed by what is false within.*
>> (Modern Love)

Tragic heroes such as Macbeth and Hamlet do have something "false within." It is after all the definition of a tragic character that his fate lies in himself and in his own weakness. Romeo and Juliet are thus not strictly speaking tragic characters, since they are betrayed by what is false without. They are the epitome of youth awakening to life, joy, love and fidelity. Theirs is the tragedy of circumstance, which perhaps makes it all the more poignant. Is it youth betrayed by age or love destroyed by hate? I think that both these are simplifications. It is true that they are victims of a family feud, but as the play unfolds one sees everything

that happens as a series of fatal accidents. We are never told the cause of the "ancient grudge" between the Capulets and the Montagues, which the Chorus refers to at the very beginning of the play. It is accepted as a fact that the servants of the two houses, as well as the young bloods, should be ready to be at each others' throats. But we don't feel that this "ancient grudge" is past remedy. After the opening brawl has been put down by Escalus, the Prince of Verona, Old Montague, who is Romeo's father, asks *"Who sets this ancient quarrel new abroach?"* (1.1.94) Lady Montague is concerned for Romeo's safety:

> *O, where is Romeo? Saw you him today?*
> *Right glad I am he was not at this fray.*
>> (1.1.106–107)

Capulet also appears to be concerned with keeping the peace. He refuses to let Tybalt attack the masked gate-crasher at the feast. But what we now call the collision course is already set in motion. The background of explosive anger and danger is an essential part of it, as is the heat of Verona and the high spirits of its youth, whether picking quarrels or falling in love.

I was fortunate enough to attempt Juliet

Painting of Peggy Ashcroft by Ethel Gabain, 1935

three times in the theatre and a fourth on radio. The first time was when I was twenty-three in John Gielgud's first-ever production. . . .

My first attempt at Juliet was inevitably agonising as I was plagued by the idea of it being "a great tragic role." I learnt after that production . . . that it is essential for Juliet to be a child of fourteen. If that is credible, then her awakening, her passion, her refusal to compromise and, finally, her tragedy take care of themselves. . . .

I know it has been said that Juliet is an impossible part to play because by the time an actress is experienced enough to play her, she's too old to look the part. I really think that is nonsense. An actress up to twenty years older than Juliet, if she is really capable of playing the part, is not too old to be convincing. Of course a very young girl, especially on the screen, will be at a great advantage, but she has to encounter a number of technical difficulties. These difficulties are, I would say, two-fold. Firstly, she has to be able to sustain a very long and demanding part on the stage. Secondly, she has to deal at times with extremely complicated verbal fireworks. The part is all simplicity, whereas the language is often complex in the extreme. ■

Why does Ashcroft believe that Romeo and Juliet are not "strictly speaking tragic characters"? To what extent do you agree with her? Explain.

Explain fully the difficulties of playing the character of Juliet. Does the character of Romeo pose similar problems? Explain.

Related Readings

by John Wain

Juliet and her nurse

In this poem, novelist, poet, and Shakespeare critic John Wain
develops an interesting contrast between Juliet and her nurse.

Under the hot slanting Italian sun,
two woman-shapes.

This one casting a lean upright shadow:
that one casting a soft rounded shadow.

Here, all quickness, insistence:
there, a habit of circling.

And why should she not circle?
She ranges for nourishment far distant.

Her landscape lies spread beneath the crags
where she sits memoried, brooding: she sails out
on broad dusty wings now and then,
to look it over.

And why should she not be insistent?
(She, she: haec, illa: our tongue does not say it.)
Needs newly awakened are needles.
One night in his arms is a down payment:
the rest is to come soon, it must come, it must.

They are like water:
this one leaping from the rock, unwarmed, unstained,
exclaiming in diamond spray, avid for contact,
contact with stone, wood, air, clay, skin,
with the throats of animals and men:

that one broadened out, standing,
in places very deep, calm on the surface,
in places shaded by old trees.

The young woman is hungry.
She wants love, which is to say she wants suffering,
joy, fury, repletion and forgiveness.
She wants to throw herself over the steep rocks.

The old woman is satisfied:
her body moves slowly and needs little,
stored with the rich protein of her memories.

Memories of when she, too,
cast a lean upright shadow:
when she threw herself over the steep rocks
and he was standing below, eager, and caught her.

The young woman will not be caught.
Down the rock-face dashes the clear water
unwarmed, unstained, wasted:
no old trees will shade her,
there will be no quiet depths.
We know the story.

Wain develops a contrast between Juliet and her nurse in terms of shadows, land-scapes, and water. Create a poster that illustrates the differences between the two women. Use pictures from magazines or original artwork.

Write your own poem in which you contrast two other characters from the play, for example, Romeo and Friar Laurence, Paris and Capulet, or Mercutio and Benvolio.

by Sarojini Shintri

Lady Capulet:
A "Neglected" Mother

What role does Lady Capulet play in the tragedy of
Romeo and Juliet? *In this selection, Shintri explores why*
Shakespeare portrays Lady Capulet the way he does.

The character of Lady Capulet appears to be rather wooden and lifeless. And the reason seems to be that Shakespeare has paid her just the attention that a character introduced mainly for its dramatic use requires.

When she is disclosing Paris's proposal to Juliet, she does not express that natural joy which usually mothers feel at their daughter's engagement. She does it as she might narrate a long story with little interest in it:

LADY CAPULET: Marry, that "marry" is the very theme
   I came to talk of. Tell me, daughter Juliet,
   How stands your disposition to be married?
JULIET: It is an honour that I dream not of.
NURSE: An honour? Were not I thine only nurse,
   I would say thou hadst sucked wisdom from thy teat.
LADY CAPULET: Well, think of marriage now. Younger than you,
   Here in Verona, ladies of esteem,
   Are made already mothers. By my count,
   I was your mother much upon these years
   That you are now a maid. Thus then in brief:
   The valiant Paris seeks you for his love.
NURSE: A man, young lady! Lady, such a man
   As all the world — why he's a man of wax.
LADY CAPULET: Verona's summer hath not such a flower.
NURSE: Nay, he's a flower, in faith — a very flower.
LADY CAPULET: What say you? Can you love the gentleman?
   This night you shall behold him at our feast.
   Read over the volume of young Paris' face,
   And find delight writ there with beauty's pen. (1.3.66–85)

It is the nurse who is excited, not Lady Capulet. And even later, when she is disclosing to her daughter the date fixed for her wedding with Paris, we see the same tediousness and lack of life and energy:

> LADY CAPULET: Well, well, thou hast a careful father, child,
>   One who to put thee from thy heaviness,
>   Hath sorted out a sudden day of joy
>   That thou expects not nor I looked not for.
> JULIET: Madam, in happy time! What day is that?
> LADY CAPULET: Marry, my child, early next Thursday morn
>   The gallant, young and noble gentleman,
>   The County Paris, at Saint Peter's Church,
>   Shall happily make thee there a joyful bride.   (3.5.111–119)

When Juliet refuses to get wed and begs of her to get it postponed, she hardly makes an effort to understand her daughter's feelings:

> LADY CAPULET: Here comes your father. Tell him so yourself,
>   And see how he will take it at your hands.   (3.5.128–129)

And when Capulet is all fire and brimstone for Juliet, she is a silent spectator, except for "You are too hot" (3.5.184).

Here Shakespeare's intentions appear to be to aggravate the tragedy by making us feel how lonely Juliet was in her troubles. And it is quite possible that Lady Capulet, having been herself brought up in a conventional atmosphere, and then again ruled by her turbulent husband, could not understand Juliet's "rebellious" nature; though it is equally possible that she did not appreciate her daughter's feelings to postpone the wedding as she did not know the reason behind it. Perhaps she was as anxious and eager as her lord to see her married well. . . .

It appears that Shakespeare was so engrossed with the young lovers and their star-struck fortunes that he did not find time enough to give due attention to Lady Capulet. She is a "neglected" mother.

Shintri views Lady Capulet as being an incomplete character. Do you agree that Lady Capulet is a "neglected" character? What aspects of her character do you think are revealed in this play? Explain fully.

Why does Shakespeare not show us any scenes in which Romeo appears with his parents? What do you think Romeo's home life is like?

Related Readings

Soft—Soft—She Breathes

by David Garrick

Actor David Garrick did more to revive interest in Shakespeare than any other person in dramatic history. He was considered the foremost Shakespearean actor of his time, and produced popular versions of the Bard to enthusiastic audiences. Garrick's versions retained much of Shakespeare's original poetry, but scenes and dialogue were added to make the plays more accessible. He introduced his adaptation of Romeo and Juliet *in 1748, and it was this version that was used for almost one hundred years. Because of the dramatic potential of having Juliet awaken and Romeo die in her arms, actors preferred Garrick's "improvements."*

ROMEO: . . . Soft—soft—she breathes, and stirs! *[Juliet wakes.]*

JULIET: Where am I? defend me, powers!

ROMEO: She speaks, she lives; and we shall still be blessed!
　　My kind propitious stars overpay me now
　　For all my sorrows past—rise, rise my *Juliet,*
　　And from this cave of death, this house of horror,
　　Quick let me snatch thee to thy *Romeo's* arms,
　　There breathe a vital spirit in thy lips,
　　And call thee back to life and love!　　　*[Takes her hand.]*

JULIET: Bless me! how cold it is! who's there?

ROMEO: Thy husband.
　　It is thy *Romeo,* love; raised from despair
　　To joys unutterable! quit, quit this place,
　　And let us fly together— *[Brings her from the tomb.]*

JULIET: Why do you force me so—I'll never consent—
　　My strength may fail me, but my will's unmoved,—
　　I'll not wed *Paris,*—*Romeo* is my husband—

ROMEO: Her senses are unsettled—restore 'em, Heaven!
　　Romeo is thy husband; I am that *Romeo,*
　　Nor all the opposing powers of earth or man,
　　Can break our bonds, or tear thee from my heart.

JULIET: I know that voice—Its magic sweetness wakes
　　My tranced soul—I now remember well
　　Each circumstance—Oh my lord, my *Romeo!*
　　Had'st thou not come, sure I had slept for ever;
　　But there's a sovereign charm in thy embraces
　　That can revive the dead—Oh honest *Friar!*
　　Dost thou avoid me, *Romeo?* let me touch
　　Thy hand, and taste the cordial of thy lips—

Related Readings

You fright me—speak—Oh let me hear some voice
Besides my own in this drear vault of death,
Or I shall faint—support me—

ROMEO: Oh I cannot,
I have no strength, but want thy feeble aid,
Cruel poison!

JULIET: Poison! what means my lord? Thy trembling voice!
Pale lips! and swimming eyes! death's in thy face!

ROMEO: It is indeed—I struggle with him now—
The transports that I felt, to hear thee speak,
And see thy opening eyes, stopt for a moment
His impetuous course, and all my mind
Was happiness and thee; but now the poison
Rushes thro' my veins—I've not time to tell—
Fate brought me to this place—to take a last,
Last farewell of my love and with thee die.

JULIET: Die! was the *Friar* false?

ROMEO: I know not that—
I thought thee dead; distracted at the sight,
(Fatal speed) drank poison, kissed thy cold lips,
And found within thy arms a precious grave—
But in that moment—Oh—

JULIET: And did I wake for this!

ROMEO: My powers are blasted.
'Twixt death and love I'm torn—I am distracted!
But death's strongest—and must I leave thee, *Juliet?*
Oh cruel cursed fate! in sight of heaven—

JULIET: Thou rav'st—lean on my breast—

ROMEO: Fathers have flinty hearts, no tears can melt 'em.
Nature pleads in vain—Children must be wretched—

JULIET: Oh my breaking heart—

ROMEO: She is my wife—our hearts are twined together—
Capulet, forebear—*Paris*, loose your hold—
Pull not our heart-strings thus—they crack—they break—
Oh *Juliet! Juliet!* [Dies.]

JULIET: Stay, stay, for me, *Romeo*—
A moment stay; fate marries us in death,
And we are *one*—no power shall part us. [Faints on Romeo's body.]

In groups, prepare presentations or create videos of Garrick's version and Shakespeare's original ending. Which do you think works better? Which did you prefer preparing and presenting? Why?

If you were directing *Romeo and Juliet,* would you consider including Garrick's "improvements"? Why or why not? Develop an argument for their inclusion.

Wherefore Art Thou Palestinian?

by Jeffrey Bartholet

The story of Romeo and Juliet *is said to have originated in fifth-century Greece. Since then, it has been retold countless times in various settings. Perhaps this story continues to be popular because it provides hope that walls can come down between warring parties.*

Two households, both alike in dignity,
(In fair Verona, where we lay our scene)
From ancient grudge, break to new mutiny,
Where civil blood makes civil hands
*   unclean.*   (Prologue, 1–4)

Fair Verona? Let's face it: Jerusalem is a far more suitable setting for *Romeo and Juliet,* Shakespeare's tragedy of passion and blood feud. And who better to play the Montagues and Capulets than Arabs and Jews? A joint production in Jerusalem is doing just that: it opens this week, with a Palestinian playing Romeo and an Israeli Jew as Juliet. "Shakespeare wrote this play about Jerusalem," says Eran Baniel, the Jewish half of an Arab-Israeli directing team. "Verona was a computer mistake." . . .

At least nobody will have trouble telling the Montagues from the Capulets: one family speaks Arabic, the other Hebrew. (English subtitles will be projected above the stage.) Some characters—such as the Prince of Verona, a kind of arbiter—use both Arabic and Hebrew, depending upon the circumstances. Delicate decisions on usage were made line by line. "We were negotiating all the time," says Fouad Awad, the Palestinian director.

The hope, of course, is that a successful production of *Romeo and Juliet* will be the seed of something larger. "As artists, we need the courage to be out in front, to show people what is good and bad," says Awad. But in a land where some opinions were formed thousands of years ago, erasing ancient grudges is a tall order. Even liberal-minded members of the audience, accustomed to the . . . bloodshed between Arab and Jew, may flinch when knives are drawn onstage. Others may feel threatened by a Palestinian kiss or a Jewish caress. The banishment of Romeo will resonate deeply for Palestinians who have seen friends or relatives deported by Israel. Not everyone will interpret the play as intended: an anonymous caller recently threatened Baniel, the Jewish director, saying his life was in danger because the play was "encouraging inter-marriage between Jews and Muslims." ■

Using the library or the Internet, research the follow-up to this June 1994 news story.

Imagine you are a drama reviewer for a newspaper or a television news program and that you have just attended a performance of this production. Write a review of the production.

based on a work
by Anna Jameson

Juliet

In her work on Shakespearean heroines, Jameson says that "it is not without emotion" that she attempts to comment on the character of Juliet. "Such beautiful things have already been said of her—only to be exceeded in beauty by the subject that inspired them! It is impossible to say anything better; but it is possible to say something more."

O Love, thou teacher,
   O Grief, thou tamer,
   and Time, thou healer of human hearts,
bring hither all your deep and serious revelations!

Rich fancies of unbruised, unbowed youth,
   visions of long-perished hopes,
   shadows of unborn joys,
   gay colourings of the dawn of existence!

Whatever memory
   of bright and beautiful in nature or in art;
all soft and delicate images,
all lovely forms,
divinest voices and entrancing melodies,
gleams of sunnier skies and fairer climes,
   Italian moonlights,
   and airs that breathe of the sweet south,
now, if it be possible, revive to my imagination —
   live once more to my heart!

Come thronging around me,
   all inspirations that wait on passion,
         on power,
         on beauty;

give me to tread, not bold,
   within the inmost sanctuary of Shakespeare's genius,
   in Juliet's moonlight bower

Jameson refers to Love as a teacher and to Grief as a tamer. What do you think she means by this? Write a poem or short paragraph in which you explore and express the implications of her statement.

ALBERT, *the Perfect Waiter*

by Bert Almon

*There is something admirable about someone who can quote
Shakespeare at appropriate moments. After reading this poem,
you may be tempted to memorize a little Shakespeare.*

Albert has left San Remo
(classical music and Italian prints)
for the kitsch of the Boar's Head Inn
with its plastic armor and gas logs
blazing heartily in the fireplace

Perhaps he's looking for his century
Albert was the perfect servant
discreet and unobtrusive
I began to think he'd trained for it
and taken Albert as a stage name

He had only one starring moment
Seeing you he dropped to his knees
and said, *If I profane
with my unworthiest hand
this holiest shrine —*
And you replied, *Good pilgrim
you do wrong your hand too much*

And so I value Albert
Look how skillfully
he has seated you in this poem
and lit the candles of romance
If I falter he'll be back
to pour a little wine
in this pilgrim's glass

Choose a quotation from anywhere in the play and incorporate it into a poem of your
own. You may imitate Almon's poem if you wish.

Related Readings

by Richard Armour

A FAMILY FEUD

This is an excerpt from the story Romeo and Juliet *as you have never read it before. To Richard Armour, nothing is sacred—including the Bard!*

Some unfortunate swordplay

Tybalt, a hot-headed Capulet, is spoiling for a fight. It's a warm day, and, with no refrigeration, nothing keeps very well. Meeting Benvolio and Mercutio in the public square, Tybalt stands fast[1] and exchanges insults with them, at the current rate. But he is really much more interested in insulting Romeo, who at this moment arrives.

"Thou art a villain," Tybalt snarls unsmilingly. This is pretty strong language, and Romeo should take umbrage.[2] But, remembering that he is now related to Tybalt by marriage, he replies politely. He realizes that you have to put up with a good deal from in-laws.

"Tybalt, you rat-catcher!"[3] Mercutio says colorfully, whipping out his sword.

"I am for you!" cries Tybalt, trying to mix him up, really being against him.

As they fight, Romeo steps between them, his courage matched only by his stupidity. Tybalt thrusts under Romeo's arm and stabs Mercutio and flies. We are not told what happened to the flies, but Mercutio is in a bad way.

"I am hurt," he groans, in one of the greatest understatements in all Shakespeare.

"Courage, man, the hurt cannot be much," says Romeo, who fails to notice that his friend is standing up to his ankles in blood.

Not until Mercutio is dead does Romeo appreciate the seriousness of the situation. Then he vows to get back at Tybalt[4] for his underhanded underarm thrust. Completely forgetting about Tybalt's being a relative on his wife's side, Romeo unsheathes, feints, parries, and thrusts. "Tybalt falls," we are told, and in a Shakespearean tragedy this usually means he is dead, which turns out to be the case.

Romeo could be executed for this act of passion, but Benvolio pleads with the Prince, who lets Romeo off easy, merely banishing him for life. To a home-town boy, who believes there is no place like Verona, this is the end.[5]

Things are a mess

That night Juliet is waiting impatiently for Romeo to come climbing up the rope, hand over hand, and ready to hand over

---

1. This is done by marking time at the double.
2. Perhaps he does, deep down inside where it isn't visible.
3. The equivalent of the modern dog-catcher, or man-with-the-net. Anyhow, it's good to know that Tybalt is employed.
4. Who has returned to the scene, probably to retrieve his sword, which he left sticking in Mercutio.
5. There are, however, three and a half acts still to come.

herself. She thinks happily of their life together, and dreams up an unusual way to memorialize her husband.

"When he shall die," she muses sentimentally, "take him and cut him out in little stars." Apparently she can see herself with a cookie cutter, and bits of Romeo all over the place. She has quite an imagination.

Just then the Nurse arrives with the news that Romeo has killed her kinsman, Tybalt, and been banished. At first Juliet shrieks piteously to learn that Tybalt has been slain, and by her husband of all people. She ransacks her vocabulary for suitable epithets to describe Romeo.

"O serpent heart, hid with a flowering face!" she screams, remembering the time he wriggled up the trellis with a long-stemmed rose in each nostril.

But her mood changes. A shudder goes through her frame. She blanches, clutches her breast, and staggers upstage left.

"Some word there was, worser than Tybalt's death," she says to the Nurse, lapsing into the grammar of her age.[6] Before the Nurse can tell her what it was, she remembers. It was "banished." The tears gush forth more violently than ever, but now in Romeo's direction. After all, she has several cousins but only one husband. Subsiding, Juliet tells the Nurse to give Romeo a ring. Since there are no telephones, the poor old soul has to shuffle the weary miles to Friar Laurence's cell, where Romeo is hiding.

Romeo is blue about his banishment,[7] but cheers up when the Nurse arrives with word that Juliet still loves him, though he must promise never to do anything like that to Tybalt again. He is further cheered when the Friar says that if he will lie low in Mantua for a while, the news of his marriage can be broken gently to old Capulet, who will welcome his son-in-law back with open arms.[8] Friar Laurence is president of the Optimist Club of Verona.

Romeo returns for one almost idyllic night with Juliet before he hies himself to Mantua. It might have been perfect, indeed, but for a small disagreement. They hear a bird singing, and Juliet says it's a nightingale in a pomegranate tree, while Romeo insists it's a lark in the poison ivy. They argue about this until dawn, and Romeo might have been caught with his ladder down had not the Nurse come in.

> At first Juliet shrieks piteously to learn that Tybalt has been slain, and by her husband of all people. She ransacks her vocabulary for suitable epithets to describe Romeo.

---

6. Fourteen.
7. And not helped any by the good Friar's remark, "Thou art wedded to calamity," a tactless thing to say to a bridegroom, whatever he may think of the bride.
8. Firearms, perhaps.

"The day is broke," she announces, slaughtering the King's Italian. Romeo takes one last kiss (for the road) and is on his way to Mantua.

Just as things seem to be taking a turn for the better, Juliet gets some bad news. Her mother brings word that she is to marry the County Paris next Thursday.

Juliet is aghast, and feels very little better when she learns that County Paris is only one man. She vows she will not marry him, come Hell or high water, both of which at the moment seem unlikely. What does come is her father, old Capulet, and when he hears that Juliet won't have Paris, he is furious.

"You baggage!" he cries, swearing he will put handles on her and carry her to church himself, if necessary. Then he gets even uglier. "I will drag thee on a hurdle thither."[9]

> Just as things seem to be taking a turn for the better, Juliet gets some bad news. Her mother brings word that she is to marry the County Paris next Thursday.

"Fie, fie!" interjects Lady Capulet, whose language is refined and monosyllabic.

"You green-sickness carrion! You tallow-face!"[10] Capulet shouts, reaching a crescendo of paternal enthusiasm, and more than a little proud of his vocabulary. "Fettle your fine joints 'gainst Thursday next," he says, thinking some deep-knee bends might limber her up. Finally he storms out in a high dudgeon, pulled by two white horses, maintaining that Juliet must marry Paris or else. The alternative is too terrible to relate.

"Do as thou wilt," says Lady Capulet, washing her hands of the affair, and toweling briskly.

But does Juliet wilt? No. She has a lot of spunk, that girl. Things look black, but she will go to Friar Laurence. *He* will know what to do. ◼

---

9. He doesn't specify high hurdle or low, but either would do.
10. Juliet still hasn't removed that cold cream.

In retelling the story of Romeo and Juliet, Armour utilizes a series of puns and wordplays. Choose three puns that you think are especially clever. Choose another three that you would classify as "groaners." Explain any two puns of your choice.

Write to Richard Armour expressing your opinion as to the value of his work being used in a classroom setting.

❦ romeo and juliet ❧

by Mark Knopfler

The names "Romeo" and "Juliet" have entered our vocabulary and have inspired ballets, operas, and even rock songs. The rock group Dire Straits produced this song in 1980.

a lovestruck romeo sings a streetsuss
  serenade
laying everybody low with a lovesong that
  he made
finds a convenient streetlight steps out of
  the shade
says something like you and me babe how
  about it?

juliet says hey it's romeo you nearly gimme
  a heart attack
he's underneath the window she's singing
  hey la my boyfriend's back
you shouldn't come around here singing up
  at people like that
anyway what you gonna do about it?

> juliet the dice were loaded from the start
> and i bet and you exploded in my heart
> and i forget i forget the movie song
> when you gonna realise it was just that
>   the time was wrong juliet?

come up on different streets they both were
  streets of shame
both dirty both mean yes and the dream
  was just the same
and i dreamed your dream for you and now
  your dream is real
how can you look at me as if i was just
  another one of your deals?

when you can fall for chains of silver you
  can fall for chains of gold
you can fall for pretty strangers and the
  promises they hold

you promised me everything you promised
  me thick and thin
now you just say oh romeo yeah you know
  i used to have a scene with him

> juliet when we made love you used to cry
> you said i love you like the stars above
>   i'll love you till i die
> there's a place for us you know the movie
>   song
> when you gonna realise it was just that
>   the time was wrong juliet?

i can't do the talk like they talk on tv
and i can't do a love song like the way it's
  meant to be
i can't do everything but i'd do anything for you
i can't do anything except be in love with you

and all i do is miss you and the way we
  used to be
all i do is keep the beat and bad company
all i do is kiss you through the bars of a
  rhyme
julie i'd do the stars with you any time

Repeat second refrain.

a lovestruck romeo sings a streetsuss
  serenade
laying everybody low with a lovesong that
  he made
finds a convenient streetlight steps out of
  the shade
says something like you and me babe how
  about it?

What do the Romeos and Juliets in Shakespeare's and Knopfler's versions have in common? How are they different?

Create a rock video or a rock video script for this song. Dire Straits produced a video for this song. If you can obtain a copy, view it and then write a short paragraph expressing your opinion of the video.

Related Readings

by Dora Jane Hamblin

NEW CAREER *for* JULIET

Advice to Other Lovelorns

Did you know that people write letters to Juliet asking for advice?
What's more, she writes back!

Juliet Capulet, while not exactly alive and well in Verona, gets 400 to 500 lovelorn letters a month. Hardly an Ann Landers volume of mail, but enough to need the services of a secretary. She get letters like this:

Dear Juliet:

I am turning to you because you are the symbol of eternal love. Thus you may be able to understand me. I am Serghej G. of Ljubljana. I am madly in love with a girl, but our parents cause trouble. One night I went out of the house to walk in the fresh snow and wanted to kill myself. Then I thought of you, and all of a sudden my life seemed more beautiful. If you can, write me a word to console me. . . .

Dear Juliet:

I am Jennifer, 14 years old, and I am in love with a boy but I don't know if he loves me. I changed my hair today, before I went to school, and he said "You seem different." Does that mean he loves me? Please reply at once. I found your address in a literature book. . . .

William Shakespeare's "literature book," and the agonies of young love, produce letters in a rainbow of scripts and languages, and some weary *postino* at the Verona post office gathers them up and delivers them to the city hall.

There for the past several months a tall, clear-eyed economics student named Paola Sella has taken them home to answer in her spare time. She has become the unpaid, unofficial "secretary to Juliet," as she signs her replies.

No one in Verona remembers exactly when the letters began to come, but they began to be answered in 1937. That was the year the city council of Verona neatened up a crypt in an abandoned Franciscan convent and installed in it a stone sarcophagus which resembles a watering trough but which had been revered for centuries as "Juliet's tomb."

As custodian of the tomb, the city installed Ettore Solimani, a sober man with the outward bearing of a ferocious shrine guard and the inner soul of a Romeo. In those days many letters were directed to "the tomb of Juliet," and Solimani took it upon himself to answer as many as he could. He wrote slowly, painfully, by hand and almost always in Italian, though occasionally he would find university students to help him with the mysteries of foreign languages. For 40 years he signed himself modestly *"la segretaria di Giulietta."*

Last autumn Solimani died, and his unseen, unknown service to the world's lovers was revealed when the *postino* could no longer deliver the letters to the tomb. The new custodian wasn't interested, and the *postino* in desperation took the letters to city hall. There Signorina Sella, who helps out with the annual theatrical and operatic productions in Verona's Roman arena, surveyed the accumulating heap of wistful correspondence and decided to look it over. I met her one day just outside the arena, and asked how she was coping with the job.

"I've not had courage to answer many," she said, sipping her mineral water. "It is a heavy responsibility because they speak, they ask, of love . . . of life. . . . " She was worried that the bulk of the letters came from the United States and Germany and she could reply in neither language.

Lately, however, Juliet's secretary has found *coraggio*. She has found university friends to help her with English and German, and a stern point of view which has short shrift for "Italian jokers," like the boy who wrote asking Juliet where on earth Romeo managed to find poison in Mantua. "I seek and find none," he complained. Signorina Sella didn't deign to reply. "Better he shouldn't find," she says.

She cherishes instead letters like the one from a 70-year-old American widow. "Dear Juliet: My pain is immense, but I don't wish to be consoled. . . . In the insupportable silence I recall your 'gentle night . . . give me my Romeo. . . . ' "

"When my parents are in bed and I sit down at my desk to answer the letters, I feel useful to someone," says Paola Sella. "I feel near the whole world, and I have the impression that I am helping to break that ugly circle of solitude which separates one person from another."

So *salve* and *evviva*, love is triumphant in Verona. ■

Write a series of letters to, and replies from, Juliet. Try to remain faithful to Shakespeare's characterization of Juliet.

Write a letter to Paola Sella expressing how you feel about her writing Juliet's replies to letters from the lovelorn. Mail the letter and wait for a reply.

Related Readings

by Karel Čapek

Romeo and Juliet

In this selection, Karel Čapek gives us another version of what really happened in the story of the famous lovers.

A young English gentleman, Oliver Mendeville, who was making the grand tour in Italy, received news in Florence that his father, Sir William, had departed this life. Sir Oliver therefore bade farewell with a heavy heart and many tears to Signorina Maddalena, promising to come back as soon as he could, and set out with his servant on the road to Genoa.

On the third day of their journey they were overtaken by a heavy downpour of rain just as they were riding into a poor and scattered hamlet. Sir Oliver halted his horse under an ancient elm.

"Paolo," he said to his servant, "find if there is an *albergo* here where we can shelter till the storm has passed."

"For your servant and horses," said a voice above his head, "the inn is yonder round the bend in the road. But you, *cavaliere*, would do great honour to my house if you would shelter beneath its humble roof."

Sir Oliver doffed his broad-brimmed hat and looked up at the window from which a fat old priest was smiling merrily down at him.

"*Vossignoria reverendissima,*" he said politely, "you show too much kindness to a stranger who is leaving your lovely country with a heavy debt of gratitude for all the goodness which has been heaped upon him so bounteously."

"*Bene,* dear son," answered the priest, "but if you go on talking a moment longer you will be wet to the skin. Be good enough to dismount from your horse and give your cloak a bit of a shake; it's raining very hard."

Sir Oliver was surprised when the *molto reverendo parocco* came out into the passage to meet him; he had never seen such a small priest before; when he bowed he had to bend so low that the blood flowed into his head.

"That will do," said the priest. "I am only a Franciscan, *cavaliere*. They call me Padre Ippolito. *Hé*, Marietta, bring sausage and wine. This way, sir, it's terribly dark just here. You are *Inglese*, is it not so? There, you see, since you English broke away from the holy church of Rome there are swarms of you in Italy. I understand, *signore*. You must be homesick for it. Poor boy, so young and an Englishman already! Cut yourself some of this sausage, *cavaliere*, it is genuine Veronese. I always say there is nothing like Veronese sausage for bringing out the flavour of wine, let the Bolognese stuff themselves with their mortadello if they like. You stick to Veronese sausage and salted almonds, my dear son. Have you been in Verona? No? A pity. It was the birthplace of the divine Paolo Veronese, signore. I am a native of Verona myself. A famous city, sir. They call it the city of the Scaligeri. Is this wine to your taste?"

"Grazie, Padre," stammered Sir Oliver. "In England we call Verona the city of Juliet."

"Fancy that," said Padre Ippolito surprised, "and why? I didn't even know that a Princess Juliet lived there. But of course I haven't been there for over forty years. Which Juliet would that be?"

"Juliet Capulet," Sir Oliver explained. "You see we have a play about her—by a man called Shakespeare. A beautiful play. Do you know it, Padre?"

"No. But wait a minute. Juliet Capulet, Juliet Capulet," murmured Padre Ippolito, "I ought to know her. I used to be at the Capulets' place with Father Laurence."

"You knew Friar Laurence?" exclaimed Sir Oliver.

"Of course I knew him! Why, I was his server. Listen, would it be the Juliet who married Count Paris? I knew her. A most pious and excellent lady, the Countess Juliet. She was a Capulet by birth, one of the Capulets who had the velvet business."

"That can't be the one," declared Sir Oliver. "The real Juliet died while still a girl in the most touching manner that you can imagine."

"Aha," said the *molto reverendo*, "then it wasn't the same one. The Juliet I knew married the Count Paris and had eight children by him. A model and virtuous wife, young sir, may God give you one like her. It's true there was a rumour that before that she had lost her head about some young scapegrace—Eh, *signore*, isn't there something of the sort to be said about all of us? Youth, we know, is hotheaded and heedless. Be glad that you are young, *cavaliere*. Are the English all young?"

"Yes," declared Sir Oliver. "Ah, Father, we too are consumed with the same fire as young Romeo."

"Romeo?" asked Padre Ippolito, and took a pull at his wine. "I seem to know that name. Why, wasn't he that young *sciocco*, that scamp, that scoundrel of the house of Montague who stabbed Count Paris? People said it was about Juliet. Yes, that was it. Juliet was going to marry Count Paris—it was a good match, *signore*, Paris was very rich and a nice young man—but Romeo made out that Juliet was to have

"Juliet Capulet," Sir Oliver explained. "You see we have a play about her—by a man called Shakespeare. A beautiful play. Do you know it, Padre?"

married him. Such nonsense, sir," snorted the priest. "As though the rich Capulets could give their daughter to one of the Montagues, who had come down in the world. And besides, the Montagues took the side of Mantua while the Capulets were on the side of the Duke of Milan. No, no. I think the *assalto assassinatico* against Paris was just an ordinary political crime. There's politics in everything in these days, my dear son. Of course, after an outrage like that Romeo had to flee to Mantua and he never came back again."

"Oh, but that isn't true!" burst out Sir Oliver. "Forgive me, Padre, but it wasn't like that at all. Juliet loved Romeo but her parents forced her to marry Count Paris—"

"They had good reasons," agreed the old priest. "Romeo was a *ribaldo* and hand in glove with the Mantuan party."

"But before her marriage with Paris Father Laurence gave her a potion to send her into a death-like sleep," went on Sir Oliver.

"That's a lie," said Padre Ippolito sharply. "Father Laurence would never have done such a thing. But it is true that Romeo attacked Paris in the street and wounded him. Perhaps he was drunk."

"Forgive me, Father, but it was quite different," protested Sir Oliver. "What really happened was that they buried Juliet. Romeo ran Paris through with his sword and killed him on her grave—"

"Stop a minute," said the priest. "In the first place it wasn't on her grave but in the street near the monument of the Scaligeri. And, secondly, Romeo didn't pierce him to the heart but only ran him through the shoulder. It isn't as easy as all that to kill a man with your sword. Just you try it, young man."

"*Scusi,*" objected Sir Oliver, "but I saw it on the stage at the very first performance. Count Paris was really run through in the duel and died on the spot. Romeo, in the belief that Juliet was really dead, poisoned himself in her tomb. That's how it was, Padre."

"Not a bit of it," growled Father Ippolito. "He didn't poison himself. He ran away to Mantua, my friend."

"Forgive me, Padre," persisted Oliver, "I saw it with my own eyes—why, I was sitting in the front row! At that moment Juliet waked up and when she saw that her beloved Romeo was dead, she took poison as well and died."

"You've got it quite wrong," said Padre Ippolito indignantly. "I cannot think who invented these rumours. The truth is that Romeo ran away to Mantua and poor little Juliet was heartbroken about it and did try to poison herself. But it was nothing, *cavaliere*, just a piece of childishness; why, she was hardly fifteen years old. I know about it from Friar Laurence, young man; of course I was only a *ragazzo* about so high at the time," the good father held out his hand about eighteen inches from the ground. "Then they took Juliet to her aunt at Bezenzano to get well again. Count Paris went there to see her; he still had his arm in a sling and you know what happens in such cases: she fell head over ears in love with him. They were married three months later. *Ecco, signore,* that's the way things are in life. I was server at her wedding in a white *cotta.*"

Sir Oliver sat as though overwhelmed. "Forgive me, Father," he said at last, "but it's a thousand times more beautiful in the English play."

Padre Ippolito snorted. "Beautiful! I don't know what you find beautiful about two young people taking their own lives. It would have been a sad business, young man. I tell you, it is more beautiful that Juliet married and had eight children—and what children! As pretty as pictures!"

Oliver shook his head. "It's not that, dear Father; you don't know what a great love is like."

The little priest blinked thoughtfully. "A great love? I think that is when two people manage to live together in unity all through their lives . . . devotedly and faithfully . . . Juliet was a rare and noble lady, my dear sir. She brought up eight children and loved her husband devotedly to the end of her days.

"So you call Verona the city of Juliet? That is extraordinarily nice of you English, *cavaliere.* Lady Juliet was truly an excellent woman, may God grant her eternal glory."

Young Oliver pulled himself out of a fit of abstraction. "And what happened to Romeo?"

"Him? I really don't know. I did hear some rumour about him.—Ah, now I remember. He fell in love in Mantua with the daughter of some marquis or other—what was he called? Monfalcone. Montefalco, or something like that. Ah, *cavaliere,* that was what you call a great love! In the end he ran away with her or some-thing—it was a highly romantic story but I have forgotten the details; you see, it happened in Mantua. But it was supposed to be a *passione senza esempio,* an over-whelming passion, sir. At least that's what they said. *Ecco, signore,* the rain has stopped."

Sir Oliver rose to his full and embarrassing height. "You've been awfully kind, Padre. Thank you so much. Perhaps I may leave something here . . . for your poor parishioners," he stammered, reddening and stuffing a handful of *zecchini* under the edge of his plate.

"No, no," protested Padre Ippolito flap-ping his hands, "you mustn't really—all that money just for a little bit of Verona sausage!"

"Some of it is for your story," said Oliver quickly. "It was—er, it was very—I really don't know what to call it. Simply amazing."

The sun streamed in at the windows of the priest's house. ■

"You've got it quite wrong," said Padre Ippolito indignantly. "I cannot think who invented these rumours."

Write a continuation of Čapek's story. Perhaps Sir Oliver travels to Mantua and discovers more details of Romeo's life, or he returns to England and attempts to retell what he has learned about Romeo and Juliet.

In a short paragraph, comment on Padre Ippolito's opinion that the tragic story as Shakespeare tells it is not as beautiful as what, according to this story, really happened.

Related Readings

Purgatory

by Maxine Kumin

And suppose the darlings get to Mantua,
suppose they cheat the crypt, what next? Begin
with him unshaven. Though not, I grant you, a
displeasing cockerel, there's egg yolk on his chin.
His seedy robe's aflap, he's got the rheum.
Poor dear, the cooking lard has smoked her eye.
Another Montague is in the womb
although the first babe's bottom's not yet dry.
She scrolls a weekly letter to her Nurse
who dares to send a smock through Balthasar,
and once a month, his father posts a purse.
News from Verona? Always news of war.

    Such sour years it takes to right this wrong!
    The fifth act runs unconscionably long.

ROMEO AND JULIET II

by Peg Balfour

If perchance they did not die
that evening in Verona
nor dust nor stones their canopy
then Romeo grows old
wrinkled brown as riding boots
face scarred from yet
another Capulet while
fair Juliet with ample girth
walks by his side . . .
he grumbles at the sum she spent
to bolster up the balcony
he can no longer climb
she fusses mumble mumble
the children waste their time
in wanton merriment
we've spoiled them both I fear
says he: silly woman
hush your mouth
didn't we ourselves take life
        too seriously

What do the two poems seem to suggest about love, life, and happiness? To what extent do you agree with the poets?

Write your own poem that begins with the premise that Romeo and Juliet do not die "that evening in Verona."

Related Readings

by Robert Nathan

Or Else *for* Love

This is another version of what really happened to the famous lovers. There's no living "happily ever after" in this retelling either—or is there?

Act One Scene 1

[FRIAR LAURENCE *comes out on stage, and faces the audience.*]

FRIAR LAURENCE: The place is Mantua, from the looks of it—some ten years after. The time:—but what is time to Mantua? The stones have weathered the centuries, and the palaces are only a little faded. People, like stones, last out the weather, and eat their sorrows with the same appetite one century or another.

Myself? I am that Friar Laurence that married Juliet to Romeo. It all began, if you remember, in Verona—Capulet and Montague at feud, one Guelph, the other Ghibelline; and Romeo, unable to get the fair Rosaline to bed with him, what between her virtue and his reputation, loses his heart overnight to Juliet, a Capulet—and must be wed to her in secret. It was a tangled story, the way it was writ; for Tybalt, Juliet's cousin, murdered Mercutio, Romeo's friend, whom, to avenge, our Romeo slew Tybalt, and was banished from the city. Meanwhile, lest Juliet be married to the County Paris, who was her parents' choice, I made some arrangement for her to swallow down a sleeping draught and so be thought dead. I sent post-haste to Romeo to lift her from the tomb and carry her back to Mantua with him. Alas, the messenger never left Verona!—and hearing Juliet dead, as he supposed, Romeo sought a poison from an apothecary, and rushing back to

Verona at night, stole to the tomb where Juliet lay sleeping . . . a grisly tale!—as it was writ by our friend Will Shakespeare, who got it from Arthur Brooke, who in turn had it from Bandello—or perhaps Boisteau . . . how a story grows from one kiss to another! Ah well! Here's the honest truth of it; Bandello never knew that the apothecary, mixing his poisons without prescription and against the law, gave Romeo a simple powder made up of alum and bicarbonate. So there he was when Juliet awoke, with no more than a puckered mouth. Not the first man to seek a hero's death, and end up instead alive and married and headed out of town. So here we are ten years later, in Mantua. Romeo and Juliet wait out their banishment, along with Juliet's old Nurse, and myself. That should be no surprise! The Father General of our Order was glad to get me out of the way of the authorities; and I myself felt responsible for the plight of these two sad children, and therefore took upon my back, by way of penance, the burden of their exile, and have kept them company ever since, both as Confessor and man of business, keeping account both of their hearts and of their pocketbooks, these being the two things over which lovers have the least control . . . that, and the passage of time. . . .

[A man's voice is heard singing.]

> A man going home
> In the dawn of the day
> To his wife . . .
> With the white lily moon on his shoulder. . . .
> What can he say? He's older.
> A short night older.

FRIAR LAURENCE: Juliet is now twenty-four, and older than her years. Girls aged quickly in those days—and being married aged them quicker yet. Juliet was a woman at thirteen—or so we are told. "Her beauty hung upon the cheek of night like a rich jewel in an Ethiop's ear." So now it is dawn in Mantua; [ROMEO, *dressed in a long cloak, comes wearily down a narrow, mean street. He comes to a house with a balcony; he looks up at it as though he might attempt the climb.*] night's candles have gone out. The man you see—it is a man—is Romeo, coming home, not unnaturally, to Juliet. I say home— but home is truly nothing more than a shabby house; one could rather call it lodgings. Ah well. . . . Let us listen now. "How silver-sweet sound lovers' tongues by night, like softest music to attending ears."

[A woman's voice singing.]

A woman alone in her bed
With the curlers and pins in her head
In the dawn of the day
With the buttercup sun on her shoulder—
What can she say? That she's older.
A long night older.

[During this song, FRIAR LAURENCE exits. ROMEO makes a half-hearted attempt to climb to the balcony, and then gives it up. It is obviously too much for him. Instead, with a shrug, he goes in at the door.]

Act One ## Scene 2

[In her bedroom JULIET, in bed, turns ominously toward the door, as it opens. ROMEO is—how old was he when he left Verona?—still under thirty, but the look of youth has been worn thin on him. He is soberly dressed; his suit is frayed and mended; he wears a new cravat, and a rose in his buttonhole.]
[ROMEO comes in like any husband who has been out all night; and crosses hopefully—but not too hopefully—to JULIET.]

JULIET: Don't touch me!

ROMEO: But Juliet . . . !

JULIET: *[Storming out of bed.]* No, I tell you! And take your hands off me! I won't stand for it!

ROMEO: The dawn came up before I knew it.

JULIET: Then where were you, to let the night go by?

ROMEO: I was behind at cards . . . I couldn't leave. . . .
[He takes a few coins from his pocket, and holds them out to her; she slaps his hand away.]

JULIET: I waited for you—all night long.

ROMEO: Darling—it's not that late! The nightingale sang me home.

JULIET: It was the lark, and not the nightingale.

ROMEO: Believe me, love, it was the nightingale.

JULIET: On the pomegranate tree? That sings so out of tune? It was the lark. You think this gray is not the morning light? Oh, fie!

ROMEO: *[Impatiently.]* What shall I do, Juliet? I try to add to the few ducats my father sends me—the only way I know how. Is it my fault you get nothing from *your* family?

JULIET: Your fault! For being a Montague!

ROMEO: That was my parents' fault. Should they have sprinkled me a Capulet? At least, they remember me.

JULIET: *[Scornfully.]* We live on cabbages. But never say my parents have forgot me! Only last year my mother sent me her love—and a feather boa!

ROMEO: It was an old one, and the moths flew out.

JULIET: *[Near tears.]* It was her own—and all the clothes I've had, except for what I came away in.

ROMEO: And what your Nurse could pack. I came away in this, *[Pointing to his jacket.]* and that's ten years ago! You do not find that pitiful?

JULIET: It's pitiful to lie alone at night. And have no friends to visit with by day.

ROMEO: The night is made for sleeping, anyway.

JULIET: You said it differently ten years ago!

ROMEO: *[Glumly.]* I did! I did! And I've learned better since.

JULIET: Sometimes I think I would be better dead.

ROMEO: God knows, I was ready to die! That wretched apothecary cheated me!

JULIET: *[Coldly.]* At least—you can amuse yourself at cards.

ROMEO: *[Bitterly.]* Amuse myself? For a few miserable coins? God give me easement from such amusement! Juliet—I'm weary to my bones!

JULIET: And what am I to do with wearied bones?

ROMEO: Knit them together, Madam!—or crochet!

JULIET: Thank you. That is not what I married for.

ROMEO: *[Sleepily.]* What *did* you marry for?

JULIET: *[Bitterly.]* I have forgot. . . . To have a home, I think. Or else for love.

[ROMEO is asleep. JULIET wakes him.]

JULIET: Romeo!

ROMEO: *[as though he hadn't heard the last part of the remark]:* You have a home.

JULIET: These—rooms a home?

ROMEO: I'll talk to you when you're more reasonable. I'm going down to see if breakfast is ready. I've been up all night. *[He turns to go.]* Go back to bed, Julie.

JULIET: I have no proper bed!

[ROMEO looks stupidly at the bed for a moment, and then goes out.]

JULIET:

I said "or else for love."

He did not hear.

His soul has clenched itself upon an egg,
And staggers cookward. And descending sleep
Falls like a morning fog around his head.
The voice that in my childhood lit my heart,
Yawns on its way to slumber. Alas, my girl,
Verona's far away, and childhood too;
As far as yesterday.
                              The world's asleep,
And in the garden of my father's house,
The scent of jasmine mingles in the night
With flutes and fountains of the nightingales.
Lost, lost, a long time gone.
                              Ah, Romeo,
I said "or else for love."
                              God keep it so.

Curtain.

☙   ☙   ☙

Imagine that you are Romeo or Juliet. Write a letter to your parent(s) asking for forgiveness and money.

This selection comes from a full-length play in which the lovers are later forgiven by their parents. They then return to Verona where they take up residence with the Montagues. Write a scene that continues their story. Try to be consistent with the characters and situation as developed by Robert Nathan.

REVIEWERS

The publishers and editors would like to thank the following educators for contributing their valuable expertise to the development of the *Global Shakespeare Series*:

Nancy B. Alford
Sir John A. Macdonald High School
Hubley, Nova Scotia

Philip V. Allingham, Ph.D.
Golden Secondary School
Golden, British Columbia

Francine Artichuk
Riverview Senior High
Riverview, New Brunswick

Rod Brown
Wellington Secondary School
Nanaimo, British Columbia

Brian Dietrich
Queen Elizabeth Senior Secondary
Surrey, British Columbia

Alison Douglas
McNally High School
Edmonton, Alberta

Kimberley A. Driscoll
Adam Scott Collegiate
Peterborough, Ontario

Burton Eikleberry
Grants Pass High School
Grants Pass, Oregon

Gloria Evans
Lakewood Junior Secondary School
Prince George, British Columbia

Professor Averil Gardner
Memorial University
St. John's, Newfoundland

Joyce L. Halsey
Lee's Summit North High School
Lee's Summitt, Missouri

Carol Innazzo
St. Bernard's College
West Essendon, Victoria, Australia

Winston Jackson
Belmont Secondary School
Victoria, British Columbia

Marion Jenkins
Glenlyon-Norfolk School
Victoria, British Columbia

Sharon Johnston, Ph.D.
Maynard Evans High School
Orlando, Florida

Jean Jonkers
William J. Dean Technical High School
Holyoke, Massachusetts

Beverly Joyce
Brockton High School
Brockton, Massachusetts

Judy Kayse
Huntsville High School
Huntsville, Texas

Doreen Kennedy
Vancouver Technical Secondary School
Burnaby, British Columbia

Betty King
District 3
Corner Brook, Newfoundland

Ed Metcalfe
Fleetwood Park Secondary School
Surrey, British Columbia

Janine Modestow
William J. Dean Technical High School
Holyoke, Massachusetts

Mary Mullen
Morell Regional High School
Morell, Prince Edward Island

Steve Naylor
Salmon Arm Senior Secondary School
Salmon Arm, British Columbia

Kathleen Oakes
Implay City Senior High School
Romeo, Michigan

Carla O'Brien
Lakewood Junior Secondary School
Prince George, British Columbia

Bruce L. Pagni
Waukegan High School
Waukegan, Illinois

Larry Peters
Lisgar Collegiate
Ottawa, Ontario

Margaret Poetschke
Lisgar Collegiate
Ottawa, Ontario

Jeff Purse
Walter Murray Collegiate Institute
Saskatoon, Saskatchewan

Grant Shaw
Elmwood High School
Winnipeg, Manitoba

Debarah Shoultz
Columbus North High School
Columbus, Indiana

Tim Turner
Kiona-Benton High School
Benton City, Washington

James Walsh
Vernon Township High School
Vernon, New Jersey

Edward R. Wholey
Sir John A. Macdonald High School
Halifax, Nova Scotia

Garry Williamson
Murdoch Mackay Collegiate
Winnipeg, Manitoba

Beverley Winny
Adam Scott Secondary School
Peterborough, Ontario

About the Series Editors

Dom Saliani, Senior Editor of the *Global Shakespeare Series*, is the Curriculum Leader of English at Sir Winston Churchill High School in Calgary, Alberta. He has been an English teacher for over 25 years and has published a number of poetry and literature anthologies.

Chris Ferguson is the Curriculum Director for the Central Texas Tech Prep Consortium in Temple, Texas. Formerly the Department Head of English at Burnet High School in Burnet, Texas, she has taught English, drama, and speech communications for over 15 years.

Dr. Tim Scott is an English teacher at Melbourne Grammar School in Victoria, Australia, where he directs a Shakespeare production every year. He wrote his Ph.D. thesis on Elizabethan drama.

Related Readings

ACKNOWLEDGMENTS

Permission to reprint copyrighted material is gratefully acknowledged. Every reasonable effort has been made to contact copyright holders. Any information that enables the publisher to rectify any error or omission will be welcomed. Selections may retain original spellings, punctuation, and usage.

The Argument from Romeus and Juliet by Arthur Brooke. Public domain. *Light Images in Romeo and Juliet* by Caroline F.E. Spurgeon which appeared in SHAKESPEARE'S IMAGERY. Reprinted by permission of Cambridge University Press. *Who Cannot Recall* based on a work by Philarete Chasles. Public domain. *What the Moon Saw* based on a work by Hans Christian Andersen. Public domain. Excerpt from *West Side Story* by Irving Shulman. Copyright © 1961 and reprinted by permission of the author and the author's agents, Scott Meredith Literary Agency, LP, 845 Third Avenue, New York, New York 10022. *On Playing Juliet* by Peggy Ashcroft. First appeared in SHAKESPEARE IN PERSPECTIVE, Vol. 1, edited by Roger Sales. British Broadcasting Corporation, 1982, pp. 25-30. Reprinted by permission of International Creative Management. *Juliet and her nurse* by John Wain. Reproduced with permission of Curtis Brown Ltd, London on behalf of The Estate of John Wain. Copyright © John Wain 1979. *Lady Capulet: A "Neglected" Mother* by Dr. Sarojini Shintri from "Woman In Shakespeare" which appeared in RESEARCH PUBLICATION SERIES 32, Karnatak University, Dharwad, 1977. *Soft—Soft—She Breathes* by David Garrick. Public domain. *Wherefore Art Thou Palestinian?* by Jeffrey Bartholet from Newsweek, June 20, 1994, © 1994, Newsweek Inc. All rights reserved. Reprinted by permission. *Juliet* based on a work by Anna Jameson. Public domain. *Albert, the Perfect Waiter* by Bert Almon from CALLING TEXAS, Thistledown Press Ltd., 1989. *A Family Feud* by Richard Armour from TWISTED TALES FROM SHAKESPEARE of 1957 published by McGraw-Hill. Copyright © 1957 by Richard Armour. Reprinted by permission of John Hawkins, Inc. *Romeo and Juliet* Words and music by Mark Knopfler. Copyright © 1980 Straitjacket Songs Limited. Used by permission of Music Sales Limited. All rights reserved. International copyright secured. *New Career for Juliet* by Dora Jane Hamblin from SMITHSONIAN, Volume 10, Number 2, May 1979. Reprinted with permission. *Romeo and Juliet* by Karel Čapek from APOCRYPHAL STORIES translated by Dora Round. English translation copyright Dora Round. Published by George Allen and Unwin Ltd. *Purgatory* by Maxine Kumin from THE PRIVILEGE by Maxine Kumin. Copyright © 1982 by Maxine Kumin. First published by The Viking Press. Reprinted by permission of Curtis Brown Ltd. *Romeo and Juliet II* by Peg Balfour, Kitchener, Ontario, from VOICES FROM THE YELLOW HOUSE. Reprinted with permission. *Or Else for Love* by Robert Nathan from JULIET IN MANTUA by Robert Nathan. Copyright © 1966 Robert Nathan. Reprinted by permission of Alfred A. Knopf Inc.

ARTWORK

Yuan Lee: cover, 12, 34–35, 40, 60–61, 68, 82–83, 96, 104–105, 114, 124–125; Reprinted by permission of the **Folger Shakespeare Library:** title page of *Romeo and Juliet* from the Second Quarto, 1599, 6; first page of *Romeo and Juliet* from the First Folio, 1623, 7; "Two households, both alike in dignity" from *Comodiae*, 1496, 13; Cupid hoodwinked from *Minerua Britanna*, 1612, 27; medlar from *The grete herball*, 1529, 43; cockatrice from *Symbolorum et emblematum*, 1605, 76; Fortune's wheel from *The hystorye, sege and dystruccyon of Troye*, 1513, 88; mandrake from *Purgantium aliarumque*, 1574, 105; lantern from *Tutte l'opera d'architettura*, 1584, 122; **John James:** 8, from *Shakespeare's Theatre* (Simon and Schuster, 1994); **Mike Reagan:** 10; **Nicholas Vitacco:** 11, 135; **IGNITION Design and Communications:** series logo; marginal art: 14, 15, 16, 22, 49, 58, 70, 71, 121; **Thom Sevalrud:** 136; **Linda Montgomery:** 140; **Yoshi Miyake:** 144; painting of Peggy Ashcroft by Ethel Gabain, 1935, from the Royal Shakespeare Company collection with the permission of the Governors of the Royal Shakespeare Theatre: 147; **Harvey Chan:** 149; **Pierre-Paul Pariseau:** 152; **Tracey Wood:** 163; **Peter Church:** 164, 166; **Amanda Duffey:** 168.